ZODIAC

BIRMINGHAM

Edited by Simon Harwin

First published in Great Britain in 2002 by
YOUNG WRITERS
Remus House,
Coltsfoot Drive,
Peterborough, PE2 9JX
Telephone (01733) 890066

All Rights Reserved

Copyright Contributors 2002

HB ISBN 0 75433 564 X
SB ISBN 0 75433 565 8

FOREWORD

Young Writers was established in 1991 with the aim of promoting creative writing in children, to make reading and writing poetry fun.

Once again, this year proved to be a tremendous success with over 41,000 entries received nationwide.

The Zodiac competition has shown us the high standard of work and effort that children are capable of today. The competition has given us a vivid insight into the thoughts and experiences of today's younger generation. It is a reflection of the enthusiasm and creativity that teachers have injected into their pupils, and it shines clearly within this anthology.

The task of selecting poems was a difficult one, but nevertheless, an enjoyable experience. We hope you are as pleased with the final selection in *Zodiac Birmingham* as we are.

Contents

Ruth Ashman	1
Philip Bailey	1

Bartley Green Technology College

Danny Brooks	2
Sean Davis	2
Craig Pemberton	3
Jamie Jenkinson	4
Adam Dobbins	4
Matthew Richards	5
Joseph Allen	5
Charlotte Turner	6
Paul Jones	7
Danielle Muddyman	7

Edgbaston High School For Girls

Caroline Smith	8
Nicola Caton	9
Stavrini Koumi	10
Laura Brookes	10
Laura Caton	11
Joleen O'Hagan	12
Sophie Laitner	12
Jessica Marchant	13
Harriet Austin	14
Lily Parker	14
Natalie Constantine	15
Tiffany Pang	16
Suprina Palak	17
Rosamond Travers	18
Nicola James	19
Sahrish Yousef	20
Alex Prew	20
Alexandria Angell	21
Amy Moore	22

Sharanpal Nagra	23
Chloe Leadbetter	24
Camilla Walt	25
Anisha Parikh	26
Laura Evans	27
Orooj Rahber	28
Shiza Khan	29
Parvinder Marwaha	30
Becky Simm	31
Hannah Parker	32
Michél Ward	33
Miriam Namih	34
Mary Jack	35
Philippa Lilford	36
Rebecca Hobbs	36
Montserrat Thorp	37
Louise Best	38
Emma Matts	39
Charlotte Morby	39
Alex Moorhouse	40
Kellianne Bartley	41
Rachel Stacey & Katy Wright	41
Palvi Sahnam	42
Beccy Newman	42
Rebecca Milford	43
Alex Swartz	43
Charlotte Moxon	44

Golden Hillock School

Alamin Siddique	44
Tabassum Bibi	45
Arfan Zafar	45
Mahpara Kanwal	46
Kadija Yesmin	46
Ayaan Abdullahi	47
Sajida Begum	47
Shapla Begum	48

Aminur Rahman	48
Shak Shamol	49
Saeed Hussain	50
Liaquat Ali	50
Isabella Sheiybani Johnson	51
Umar Muhammed Malik	52
Kamran Abass	53
Rushia Begum	54
Noor Yasin	55
Rubel Miah	56
Sabina Ahmed	56
Mohammed Saleem	57
~~redacted~~	~~redacted~~
Anum Mahmood	58
M Qasim Rafiq	59
Magnaz Begum	60
Zahed Hussain	61

Hillcrest School For Girls

Amy Flood	61
Claire Kennedy	62
Emily Bailey	62
Sana Anwar	63
Zoe Coules	63
Elisha Huxtable	64
Kimberley Mohammed	65
Rebekah Ward	66
Cheryl Crawford	66
Sarah Isham	67
Sarah Bathgate	68
Sophie Martin	69
Stacey Graham	70
Tukyia Brown	70
Sonia Shukat	71
Rooth Georgeson-Cartwright	72
Sherrelle Williams	72
Natalie Smith	73

Roxanne Conway	73
Samantha Cox	74
Kimberley Dawes	75
Catherine Brinsdon	76
Hannah Paddock	76
Charlotte Hathaway	77
Natalie Mercier	78
Ashia Hamid	78
Fayola Lezama	79
Nicola Strolin	80
Lyndsey Smith	80
Stacey Frost	81
Jolande Allen	82
Nicola Minks	82
Laura Carty	83
Kaisha Campbell	84
Dannielle Caudy	84
Amie Herbert	85
Caroline Dunnett	86
Anna-Marie Averill	87
Emma Savage	88
Rosie Tearle	89
Faye Burrows	90
Cressida McDonnell	90

Holy Trinity RC School

Keeley Murray	91
Coan Gayle	92
Amelia Asquith	92
Ashley Newell	93
Laura Douglas	94
Nathan Burrell	94
Jerome Hall	95
Ammar Choudhry	96
Chantelle Frue	96
Daniel Gallagher	97
Kayleigh Burns	98

Anil Singh	98
John McDougall	99
Tasmira Ahmed	100
Karolis Tertelis	100
Sarah Lynch	101
Jamie Smith	102
Lauren Caballero	102
Amina Khan	103
John Claffey	104
Micheala McCalla	104
Emma White	105
James Cotter	106
Faisal Ahmed	106
Sarah-Jane Williams	107
Alex Walters	108
Lyndsey Johnson	108
Joseph Barnett	109

Josiah Mason Sixth Form College
Saima Sarwar	110
Melissa George	110

King Edward VI Five Ways School
Suzanne Atkins	111
Jodi Dixon	112
Reece Somers	113
Daniel Knowles	114
Ayaaz Nawab	114
Sally Cooper	115
Renna Mubarak	116
Harriet Smith	118
Maryam Sharif-Draper	119
Laurie Young	120
Yury Villalonga-Stanton	121
Rachel Fennell	122
Laurence Sutton	123
Ben Cryan	124

Daniel Carter	125
Mark Graham	126
Penelope Thomas	127
Giuseppe D'Amone	128
Eva Quigley	129
Peter Massey	130

King Edward VI Handsworth School

Sabina Pawar	131
Katharine Perry	132
Ayushah Khan	132
Jaspreet Bilkhu	133
Jenny Meszaros	134
Aniqa Alam	134
Kwan Yee Wong	135
Nisha Ranga	136
Oeiisha Williams	136
Rebecca Robotham	137
Jenni Bickley	138
Kavina Nijjar	138
Jenny Owen	139
Nisha Ajimal	140
Charlotte Florance	141
Emma Prendergast	142
Hannah Vawda	143
Alison Hearn	143
Jenny Tasker	144
Sinitta Flora	145
Lucy Machon	146
Annika Ranga	147

Kings Norton Girls' School

Rachel Webb	147
Kirsty Davies	148
Eleanor Browning	148
Charlotte Creba	149
Penny Bourne	150

Stephanie Smyth	151
Yasmin Fearon	152
Kelly Johnson	152
Michelle Harris	153
Elizabeth Cooke	154
Katy Proctor	154
Katy Marshall	155
Laura Carroll	156
Laura Batsford	156
Louise Colin	157
Hannah Freemantle	157
Nicola Ashmore	158
Danijela Kastratovic	158
Kellie-Marie Windsor	159
Fay Newman	160
Charlotte Burch	160
Lauren Allen	161
Elizabeth Rose	161
Laura Greenway	162
Ashleigh Devine	162
Jade Atterbury	163
Laura Preece	164
Rachel Galloway	165
Beth Hiscock	166
Rebecca Glover	166
Caroline Busby	167
Sara Hughes	168
Julia Wood	169
Natalie Heraper	170
Emma Yates	170
Acacia Dixon	171
Hayley Adams	172
Alice Jones	172
Avril Flower	173
Emma Gossage	173
Charlotte Tisdale	174
Aimee Ibbetson	174

Hayley Reeves	175
Vicky Burlison	175
Katie Freezer	176
Lauren Currier	176
Kirsty Bond	177
Laura Allsop	178
Victoria Bunting	178
Sophie Keenan	179
Jessica Pritchard	179
Yvonne Forrest	180
Rebecca Jones	180
Helen Shaw	181
Lydia Johnson	182
Alexandra Waldron	182
Laura Jones	183
Selina Abercrombie	183
Michele Prosser	184
Penny Andrea	184
Anisa Haghdadi	185
Kimberley Ohren	186
Manijeh Arabpour	187
Kerry Holohan	188
Abigail Tomlins	188
Kimberly Wellings	189
Lorna Brown	189
Amy Farrington McCabe	190
Katie Rouse	190
Katarina Jankovic	191
Rebekah Hand	192
Kelly Penman	192
Sophie Hickman	193
Charlotte O'Sullivan	194
Amy Johns	194
Louise Parks	195
Kelly Scott	196
Sarah Ventre	197
Sheryl Pagan	198

Samantha Moore	198
Chloe Amoo	199
Rachel Doherty	199
Lauren Spencer	200
Alice Ridgway	200
Sophie Lawrence	201
Emma Stiff	202
Leah Murray	202
Charlotte Williams	203
Lucy Willetts	204
Abby Field	204
Elizabeth Sanders	205
Emma Lewis	206
Leila Milne	206
Olga Milkiewicz	207
Madeleine Sanderson	207
Elizabeth Hodgkinson	208
Jessica Grant	208
Beth Collett	209
Kirsty Rostill	210
Emily Meades	210
Joanne Griggs	211
Hayley Rock	212
Sophie Hall	212
Laura Jackson	213
Laura Hardy	214
Emily Heel	214
Rebecca Farman	215
Jess Edwards	216
Kathryn Taylor	217
Rachael Priest	218
Anna Harris	218
Louisa Hitchen	219
Lorna Nickson	220
Eno Umotong	220
Katie Jowett	221
Kirsty Dodwell	222

Moseley School And Language College
- Jack Kirk — 223
- Ryasat Khan — 223
- Zakar Hussain — 224
- Lee Beasmore — 224
- Abida Butt — 225
- Akram Bahakinah — 226
- Nasir Ali — 226
- Faisal Farooqui — 227

Selly Oak School
- Jonathan Pinfield, Stephanie Smith, Darren Evans, Deepak Kaura, Sukhbir Singh, Shoib Khan, Lara Hall, Nicholas George, Sintero Clarke, Janine James & Johnathan Keogh — 228
- Shane Ashman — 229
- Paul Wright — 229

Shenley Court School
- Charlotte Holden — 230
- Rachel Williams — 230
- Jason Vigers — 231
- Richard Lynch — 231
- Billy Ashington — 232
- Anthony Palmer — 232
- David Smith — 233
- Sarah Ryan — 233
- Gemma Tierney — 234
- Sean Millard — 234
- Mark Jones — 235
- Stacey Holland — 235
- Natalie Farrell — 236
- Richard Crow — 237
- Luke Noble — 238
- Nicola Kumas — 238

Rachel Hadley	239
Nicholas Graham	239
Lisa Bick	240
Judy Malin	240
Paul Dixie	241
Anne-Marie Hockell	242
Carlie France	242
Zara Ling	243

St Paul's School For Girls

Sarah Williams	243
Cecilia Smart	244
Tiisetso Mogase	244
Stacey Winward	245
Rachael Pallett	246
Rachel Kane	246
Maria Kenny	247
Catherine Harris	248
Samantha Hawkins	248
Laura O'Brien	249
Lauren Hall	250
Kelly Wyke	250
Victoria Barnett	251
Laura Kielty	252
Ruth Guy	252
Hayley Williams	253
Kayleigh Sheridan	254
Roxanne Boothe	254
Siobhan Hussain	255
Laura Taylor	256
Clare Stajka	256
Hayley Hulme	257
Michelle Cave	258
Sally Wagstaff	258
Hannah Smith	259
Aimee Kelly	260

Stockland Green School

Lisa McCarthy	261
Nicola Groom	261
John Leachman	262
Gemma Stratford	262
Danielle Radway	263
Kimberley Bradley	264
Morgan Webley	265
Liam McGuinness	266
Sean Allen	266
Laura Higgins	267
Marteen Savory	268
Katie Fowler	268
Anton L Williams	269
Karine Stevenson	270
Shyro Lall	270
James Maiden	271

The Poems

My Diving Hero

The constant sound of guns being fired
Bombs thrown over and gas dropped down
My friends all around me, when this breaks the silence
'Get your head down and stop acting like a clown.'
He shouted and dived upon my head,
I thought, 'What ya doin'?'
Little did I know he was dead,
He took the bullet meant for me.
For the next few days I was a nervous wreck,
I hated to shoot people because . . .
Maybe I would be the one killing someone else's
Friend, brother, son, dad or just someone in lust,
Although I hardly knew Daz,
It hurt me like he'd been my brother,
But I'll always remember him as
My diving hero!

__Ruth Ashman (14)__

January

January strides through the land,
A gale whipping through his cloak,
He breathes mist
On towns and villages,
Leaving a chill in the places
Where he has been.
Snow falls from his hair,
Smothering everything,
Destroying any life,
So that it crumbles in the cruel cold.
He leaves misery behind him and
Imprisons people in a dungeon of
Ice, snow and depression.
January.

__Philip Bailey (11)__

Boring Sunday Recipe

It's meat again, same old things,
Is this all that Sunday brings?
Soggy roasters, mushy peas,
Give us something different please!

Why not chips and scrambled eggs,
Hot dogs, beans or chicken legs?
A tasty plate of noodles and rice
Would make my Sunday really nice.

Instead I sit and suffer the roast,
Wishing it was beans on toast!
Veg is pushed to the side,
Stuffing and mash desperate to hide.

So here we are with all the waste,
Scraping the gravy off like paste.
I do not know why mom still cooks,
'Cause we all think the dinner sucks.

Danny Brooks (11)
Bartley Green Technology College

Holiday Recipe

Take a blazing hot sun,
Place in the middle of the sky,
Add a mountain of sand
And pour on some water.
Whisk lightly to make frothy waves,
Decorate the sand with colourful seashells.
Sprinkle the sand with skinny and flabby bodies,
Leave to toast under the blazing sun until golden brown.

Sean Davis (11)
Bartley Green Technology College

BALL RECIPE

Football here,
Baseball there,
Golf balls right over there.

Put them in a big, big pot,
Mix them round
And add some pop.

Netball here,
Rugby ball there,
Tennis ball right over there.

Put them in a big, big pot,
Mix them round
And add some pop.

Cricket ball here,
Volleyball there,
Basketball right over there.

Put them in a big, big pot,
Mix them round
And add some apple rot.

Volleyball here,
Beach ball there,
Ping-pong ball right over there.

Put them in a big, big pot,
Mix it round
And add some apple rot.

Football here,
Baseball there,
Golf balls right over there.

Craig Pemberton (11)
Bartley Green Technology College

CHRISTMAS RECIPE

Take one large Christmas tree
And sprinkle on some glimmering tinsel.
Add a golden star on top
And a Santa here and there.
Dangle lights around the tree,
While we're waiting for Christmas,
You and *me*.
Leave out the milk and mince pies
For Santa's on his way,
And don't forget poor Rudolph,
A carrot or two for him,
And after Christmas has come,
He gets to sit around and have some *fun!*

Jamie Jenkinson (11)
Bartley Green Technology College

EXAMS

Take 1lb of English, science and maths going around in my head,
Add one spoonful of sleeping peacefully in my bed,
8oz of numbers, letters and experiments in my brain,
Add 4oz of going insane,
12oz of quietly in a room we sit.
4lbs of I'd rather be running around in my PE kit,
1½lbs of finishing the test,
6oz of my hand is glad for the rest.

Adam Dobbins (11)
Bartley Green Technology College

FOOTBALL

First you will need twenty-two players
On a grassy football pitch,
Add some goal posts,
Then there's the ball to fetch.

We nearly have a match,
There's just a few things to add,
A referee and some linesmen
And two pairs of corner flags.

Twenty thousand screaming fans
Would also be so good,
A couple of goals and penalty kick,
We'll finish it covered in mud.

Matthew Richards (11)
Bartley Green Technology College

BIRTHDAY RECIPE

Take a pinch of early awakening,
Add a teaspoon of anticipation,
Make a mixture a year older,
Mix with presents and cards,
Three tablespoons of partying.
Add a dash of fun and mix well with friends.
Serving suggestion - day trip garnish.

Joseph Allen (11)
Bartley Green Technology College

CHRISTMAS RECIPE

Stuff one oversized turkey,
Then pour everyone a large glass of wine.
Mom brings in dinner for everyone,
She makes sure it's on time.

The crispy roast potatoes,
The sloppy, lumpy mash,
The hot, runny gravy,
The fire's hot burnt ash.

The neat table with tinsel,
The party poppers popping,
The Christmas hats we are wearing,
The Christmas lights are twinkling.
Red, pink, blue and green,
Now it's time to listen to the Queen.

The children are so excited
To open all their presents,
Adults laughing and joking,
Gran's nearly choking.

Darkness has fallen,
Now it's nearly bedtime.
Everyone's nearly asleep,
Snow is falling softly,
There's not even a peep.

Charlotte Turner (11)
Bartley Green Technology College

A Football Team Recipe

On a Saturday afternoon,
In the dressing room,
Put on your boots and the rest of the kit,
Go on the pitch and fight for it.

Before kick-off do some warm-ups,
Don't talk about a bet,
At kick-off put some balls in the back of the net.

At full time shake some hands,
For the next match, go to Spain
And get some tans.

Paul Jones (11)
Bartley Green Technology College

Sunday Recipe

Put a drop of dinner,
Add no playing out,
An ironing board and an iron,
A touch of early bed.
Just don't add a drop of fun
Because it might just as well be glum.
I would throw in a drop of washing up
And cleaning up,
And a drop of homework too
And for dessert, a drop of bedroom tidying.

Danielle Muddyman (11)
Bartley Green Technology College

JUST STARS

Once space was nothing but a void,
With a few solitary stars,
Tiny pinpricks of never-ending white light.

Gradually times changed,
Space became a black infinity
With millions of constellations and lights,
But still, there were only stars out there.

Science fiction began to come into our lives,
Fantasies of planets, other worlds and races,
But still space remained a black, continuous void with
Naught but stars and planets floating aimlessly about like
 lost travellers,
No one really knew, nor cared what was out there.

Finally man made it to the moon,
Leaving a footprint as a constant reminder,
Left by a man in unfamiliar territory, an invader, as it were.
These few people watched Earth rise in the moon's airless,
 inhospitable morning.
These brave adventurers brought us pictures, photographs
And videos of incomparable beauty that no one ever thought existed,
But still, space remained a star-filled void, devoid of life in its
 inhospitable, oxygen-starved mass,
Punctuated by a few lone planets, spaceships and probes.

Finally space exploration unfolded,
We learned of things we never knew existed,
Anomalies, unidentifiable clouds, supernovas,
All beauties no science fiction programmes can show us.
Space is no longer a star-filled emptiness,
But an immeasurable blackness
With balls of intense heat and fusion as the tiny, twinkling stars,
A whole array of amazing phenomena that the human mind
Cannot even begin to comprehend.

So many of us have seen pictures of this boundless cosmos,
Not many of us will see this amazing crowded emptiness,
But we will always know that space is no longer an inky void with
A few solitary pinpricks of incessant white light we see as stars.

Caroline Smith (12)
Edgbaston High School For Girls

CRAZY COLOURS

Red:
Is summer roses,
Soft, smooth.

Orange:
Is sunny spring,
Soothing, salubrious.

Yellow:
Is bright, fresh flowers,
Spreading, scented.

Green:
Are the trees in summer,
Stately, satisfying.

Blue:
Is the night sky,
Secluded, secretive.

Indigo:
Is paint,
Solemn, soulful

Violet:
Is lavender,
Sweet, serene.

Nicola Caton (11)
Edgbaston High School For Girls

?

In the shimmering sky, on the unswept ground,
Beaming mightily, no sound, no sound.

Seeping through our thoughts and minds,
Nobody knows, they say it is blind.

Racing like a thousand stallions,
Blazing, blazing,
Galloping,
Burning.

Yet,
All alone,
In a darkened room,
Nothing stirs,
No thoughts to prune.

Is all around you, mingling above.
The feeling you yearn for,
The finest,
Love.

Stavrini Koumi (13)
Edgbaston High School For Girls

CAT

Disco divas,
School swots,
Back alley gangsters,
Mysterious monsters.

Disco divas,
Never-sleepers,
School swots,
Read books,
Get evil looks.

Back alley gangsters,
Hiding and creeping,
Mysterious monsters,
Slinking and sliding.

Your cat is one of these.

Laura Brookes (13)
Edgbaston High School For Girls

GOODBYE!

When you love someone,
Saying goodbye is hard,
The hardest thing in the world.

Like the leaves fall
From the trees
In the autumn,
Your happiness leaves you.

Like the fire dies,
Starved of oxygen,
Leaving just burnt ashes,
Your hopes are extinguished.

Like the water dries up
Causing a drought,
Killing the living,
Your heart cracks up.

When you love someone,
Saying goodbye is hard,
The hardest thing in the world.

Laura Caton (12)
Edgbaston High School For Girls

SITTING HERE

Are you going to stand and stare?
Me sitting here . . .
You standing there.
My heart, so fragile, was broken today,
And I just want you to walk away.
Can't you leave me alone?
I need my space.
Can't you see my shattered face?
It's as if you enjoy watching tears that I shed,
Tears that I cry, do they put thoughts in your head?
You standing there, a grey, lifeless stone.
So with me sitting here . . .
And you standing there . . .
If the situation reversed,
I would not be here.

Joleen O'Hagan (13)
Edgbaston High School For Girls

MY DREAM IS TO . . .

My dream is to swim with the swirling waves,
Swim with the glimmering fish.
My dream is to hear the gentle lap from the ocean's depths
On the soft, soft sand.
My dream is to see the fascinating creatures of the clear, blue ocean,
My dream is to watch the ferocious ocean predators
Patrolling the dark, murky depths.
My dream is to dive deep, deep, deep,
Down to the ocean's golden bed,
With cool water streaming through my fingers,
Escaping to a world of fantasy.

Sophie Laitner (12)
Edgbaston High School For Girls

WAITING FOR DAWN

Sitting in the dark, waiting for dawn,
Alone in the night, thinking of you.
Remembering the looks you cast my way,
Wondering why you give me such pain.

What have I done to deserve this hate?
A pure and bitter burning rage,
That eats at your heart and destroys the love
That you once had for me.

I gaze at the sky, a black velvet tent,
That covers the world and obscures my sight,
When I try to see my way back to you,
From this place so eternally dark.

I wait for the dawn to end this night,
The time when I can be free again,
Of this oppressive weight in my heart,
Free from your looks, free from your scorn.

I wonder if you, who brought this despair,
Have closed your eyes in an endless night,
While looking for stars high above,
To signal the end and to give you some hope?

For no stars shine in my sky,
Though I search so hard for them
And there is no glimmer of light
When I look between the lengthening shadows.

I'm here all alone,
In the darkness of my soul,
Looking at the sky
And waiting . . . waiting for dawn.

Jessica Marchant (13)
Edgbaston High School For Girls

MY BIGGEST QUESTION

Who am I really talking to?
Who can answer the questions I have?
So many people have nothing but love for you,
All I have is disappointment.

People trust you with their lives,
Even after their lives are worthless,
The stale thoughts run through my head,
The endless questions can never be answered.

You have such power with the love that is bestowed on you,
Fields full of trust, dedication and respect.
Have you really let me down,
Or am I just another grain?

You see what no one else can,
To the needles of our soul,
Nothing matters now,
The tapestry is finished.

Harriet Austin (15)
Edgbaston High School For Girls

COLOURS ARE . . .

Blue is:
Sky, everlasting, ever changing,
Sea, crashing, calm,
Flowers, gentle, genuine.

White is:
Clouds, wispy, whirling,
Silver stars, shiny, sparkling,
Snow, soft, simple.

Yellow is:
Fire, flickering, fragile beginning,
Sun, bright, bold,
Dandelions, small, scented.

Red is:
Anger, fury, temper,
Cherries, summery, sweet,
Jam, sticky, tasty.

Lily Parker (11)
Edgbaston High School For Girls

IT HURTS

Nobody knows how I feel,
It hurts when I see them.
Inside I'm ready to burst with a hurtful fire,
They're like a bug at the corner of my life,
Stinging me constantly,
Hurting me in the weirdest but most painful ways,
I cry,
I talk,
Nothing can remove them from my life.
I wake up day after day, hoping they will go away.
Life goes on as it never ends,
But all I can do,
What I have to do,
Is wait,
Wait for them to go
And let me be free from this nightmare.

Natalie Constantine (13)
Edgbaston High School For Girls

BOYS/GIRLS

Boys

Big ones, small ones, fat ones, thin,
Massive heads, but no brains within.
They think they're wicked with their gel in their hair,
But when your hair's nice, they don't even care.
Bulging muscles as they run in the gym,
Oh I suppose I'll go out with him.

Bringing flowers and chocolates at eight,
Doesn't make up for you being late.
He promises me a night of romance,
So he takes me to an upper school dance,
But when we get there he treads on my feet
And his dance moves are totally out of beat.

At the end of the night I want to slap his face,
Why did he take me to this awful place?
Then he smiles and expects a kiss,
What kind of idiot is this?
Do I have to say anymore?
Going out with boys is such a bore.

Girls

Some are slender, some are plump,
Some have even survived being dumped.
Some I hate and some I love,
Some are angels from above.

Some can boogie day and night,
Some can even start a fight,
Some can drink and some can drive,
Some can make me feel alive.

Some are snotty, some are fit,
Some can dance and some can hit.
Some are super, some are great,
Some I have even asked out on a date!

Tiffany Pang (12)
Edgbaston High School For Girls

MUM, DAD AND TED

My mummy always cares for me,
My mummy dries my tears,
My mummy always shares with me my
Secrets, hopes and fears.

My daddy always cuddles me,
My daddy fixes my bike,
My daddy always calls me names, like
Sweetheart, Honey and Tyke.

But when I ask my mom things like,
'Can I have some chocolate cake?'
She'll always say,
'I'm busy, ask Dad, he's outside fixing the gate.'

But then when I ask my dad,
'Can I have some chocolate cake?'
He'll say, 'I'm doing something.
Ask Mom, she's inside cooking the steak.'

Then I have to ask my teddy,
And he always says yes,
But then I end up in the kitchen
With a lot of chocolate mess!

Suprina Palak (13)
Edgbaston High School For Girls

Two Worlds

Silver shining up high in the sky,
A spaceship glides silently by.
Up beyond the realms of Earth
The comets soar and fly and swerve.

Back on Earth the problems grow,
More cars and trains each year we know.
Oil slicks kill birds and fish and seals,
Half the world has too few meals.

Space is cold and clean and clear,
This is a place where people have not interfered.
The twinkling stars in the gloomy sky,
Shine above us as we lie.

Then down on Earth more things go wrong,
As it gets less common to hear birdsong.
Endangered species don't stand a chance,
As we live our lives and do not glance
Towards the creatures suffering near,
Crying out, we do not hear.

The planets swirling, twirling round
In space no one can hear a sound.
The sun shines down, a flaming ball,
Lighting up the sky, glinting on the wings
Of aeroplanes that fly.

Back on Earth, the rich have plenty,
The poor are left with stomachs empty.
The rainforest shrinks, the glaciers melt,
In our world today, much pain is felt.

Although some of us try to do our best,
It does not make up for the rest,
Who sit around without the fear
Our world may someday disappear.

Rosamond Travers (13)
Edgbaston High School For Girls

SALCOMBE

Glistening waters like sparkling mirrors,
Magical scenes arousing minds,
Salcombe is stunning,
Its angelic atmosphere fills the air.

Subtropical climate,
Ice cream dripping,
The Salcombe Regatta,
Boats winding around creeks.

The white sails of Salcombe's yawls,
The East Portlemouth ferry,
Union Street in regatta regalia,
Sailors filling the narrow streets,
Mill Bay, Sunny Cove, filled with pin-sized dots.

Holiday homes,
Emptied and filled,
Boats stored and cleaned,
Salcombe's spirit never fails.

Nicola James (13)
Edgbaston High School For Girls

PEACE, BELIEF AND HOPE

There I lay silently asleep,
Peace of mind and everything else.
Suddenly I woke up and began to weep,
Why can't there be more time for personal peace?

I got ready
For the school was my test.
One of peace, belief and hope.

Inner peace is harmony and courage all in one,
Belief is the faith you have and the strength of your religion.
Hope is most important,
For you hope in everything.

Though only a child,
I tend to think
How precious life is,
And should consist of these three things.

Sahrish Yousef (13)
Edgbaston High School For Girls

CONTAGIOUS

Laughter and smiles are contagious,
Yawns and burps are too,
Hiccups and tears are spreading,
Whatever shall we do?

Call in the doctors!
Tip the water out of the jug,
Give them the treatment
And send out the bug!

But what about diseases,
Meningitis and the flu,
We can't cure Aids yet,
Aren't they contagious too?

Alex Prew (13)
Edgbaston High School For Girls

FENCING

Training, timing,
Lunging, winning.

Fitness, technique,
Self-discipline.

Speed, turning,
Dancing, balestra.

Fleche, movement,
Smoothness, routine.

Gliding, darting,
Lightning speed.

Hitting, masks denting,
Swords breaking.

Fearing, breathing heavily,
Nervousness, wonder.

Winning, surprise,
Piercing heat,
Relief . . .

Alexandria Angell (13)
Edgbaston High School For Girls

Autumn

Autumn is a time of change,
From summer's warmth
To winter's chill.
Leaves change from green
Through to red, to a crumbling brown,
And fall to settle
At the wind's whim.
Plants withdraw into the ground
To sleep the cold days through.

We gather warmth to us
In the autumn chill
And on come our woollies warm,
To stop the creeping fingers of the howling wind
Fires are lit,
Electric blankets switched on.

Autumn is a time of settling,
Of pulling in,
Of closing down,
Of preparing
For winter's icy breath.

But autumn is a time of colour,
Of sunlight through bare branches,
Of squirrels hoarding nuts,
Of robin redbreast,
Who shares the seasons with us,
Brightening dull days
With a flash of colour
And then surrendering to winter's icy breath.

Amy Moore (12)
Edgbaston High School For Girls

LOVING YOU

I needed to know,
I needed to see
The handsome face
Which is now beside me.

I remember the days
We spent together,
When we thought we
Would be together forever.

I think now
And wonder why
I left you
For another guy.

The last time we saw each other,
We were both in tears.
The first time we met each other,
We were talking about our fears.

I leave you now,
In heaven we shall meet,
Though not alone,
But with the love we both need.

I've got it out of my head,
I've been thinking about it for days.
When thinking, I would look up
At the sun's beautiful rays.

I hope you can forgive me
For not telling you,
I wonder what you're thinking
Maybe, I am still in love with you!

Sharanpal Nagra (13)
Edgbaston High School For Girls

THE OUTSIDER

I've always wondered why
I am the way I am
And why the way I am
Is not the way they are?

I've tried to be like them
Tried to understand
Tried to see the obvious
And tried to look beyond.

Beyond the cold exterior
To a warmth they could've shared
A warmth I longed for
But now I've lost my chance

Even though they miaow
And I bark
Even though they hiss
And I growl.

We could've worked something out
Kennel doors shouldn't stop a friendship
But these ugly great dividers
Ruined my chance of joining their pack.

But I'm off now
Off to a place
A place most kennel animals dream of reaching
Where humans call you their pet.

But I shrink into the shadows
I want to stay with my unknown friends
Hoping eventually
That the cats will accept the dog.

Chloe Leadbetter (13)
Edgbaston High School For Girls

A Crush

A crush makes you feel inside an indescribable feeling.
A tingle rushes up your spine whenever
This person crosses your mind.

When the person talks to you, another feeling takes place.
You may find yourself thinking, 'Oh heck, I look a disgrace.'
Then the person walks off and you think,
'I was such an idiot, why the hell didn't I talk to him?
Now he will think I'm just another bird.'

You're out and about and you see him again
And your head throbs out with the pain.
You try to run off, but it doesn't work
And he sees your orange mane.

He comes up close and you have the urge
To give him a kiss on the cheek, then he says the famous line . . .
'Would you like to come back to mine?'

The situation is unbelievable and you instantly say, 'Yes!'
You now feel fine and are thinking that he
Is totally and utterly divine.

You get to the flat and she is there, that enemy from around the corner.
The feelings rush and come right back, the headache,
Stomach ache and sickness.
You run off like a shot not daring to think
About what just happened with that evil girl, Jess.

Although he ripped your heart out you still have to confess
That boy you had a crush on made your life such a terrible mess.
You may be laughed at when you go to school the next day,
But that doesn't matter because you know in your heart
That boys are the ones who make all the stress!

Camilla Walt (12)
Edgbaston High School For Girls

SEASIDE

Wandering aimlessly across the golden sand,
I walked barefooted,
Sand tricking through my toes.

All was quiet but for the small waves,
In the carpet of aqua-green sea
The sea seemed calm and mysterious,
A place I did not know.

Cliffs towered high
Above the guarding shore,
Gulls swooped and cried like kittens.
Birds I could not name
Dived into the sea to hunt their prey.

Cool breeze of air ran past me as I walked,
I looked up
To see the sun sinking into the scarlet sky.
Oh how I remembered the poem
We used to say about a red sky.

I looked down into a shallow pool
To see nature's hidden treasures.
Velvet crab shredding to pieces an orange starfish,
With its razor-sharp teeth.
Urchins being obstinate and clinging to jagged rocks and pebbles,
Hermit crabs looking for a place to live.

Suddenly, I heard a clap of thunder
And a lightning strike overhead,
I knew it was time to go now,
To leave this amazing place,
Where creatures live, where birds fly,
But I knew I would come back another day.

Anisha Parikh (12)
Edgbaston High School For Girls

THAT MYSTERIOUS GIRL

Winter strikes,
The trees are bare,
You see someone walking
Without a care.

You see a young girl all in white,
Drifting between the trees.
Her face is pale and her feet are bare,
She looks and turns away.

You walk towards this mysterious girl,
And then she disappears,
You twirl around and she's there again
And starts to confirm your fears.

You back away and she follows you,
Still chanting out your dreams,
And as you run you try to contemplate
What you think it all means.

And when she's finished she vanishes,
In a split-second wisp of smoke
And even through she is finally gone,
You're left on your own to choke.

Your breath gets short,
You start to tire,
You slowly fall to the ground
And as your eyes start to get heavy,

One thought floods your mind . . .

Who was that mysterious girl,
Who's left me here to die?

Laura Evans (12)
Edgbaston High School For Girls

THE HAUNTED LIBRARIAN

The spooky librarian says to me,
'There's people waiting, can't you see?'
I huff and puff and get up from my seat,
I look around and whisper,
'God, you are a creep!'
I pack my bag and get out of there,
Then she gives me a daring stare,
All the girls start giggling at me,
They are saying, 'What kind of freak is she?'
She barks like a dog,
She looks like a hog,
What else can I say? She just ruins my day.
The library is a creepy place,
This is a fact you have to face.
The ancient shelves,
Dirty and dusty,
The iron knobs, rough and rusty,
The well-framed picture in the room
Shows my fate, which is doom.
A pencil drops on the floor,
'What's all that noise?' she begins to roar.
Her mouth is smoothly in a frown,
Her shoulders hunched, her shirt smoothed down,
You will never see happiness in my eyes,
Until the evil librarian dies.
Listen folks, beware,
Libraries can be a bit of a scare!

Orooj Rahber (12)
Edgbaston High School For Girls

DAYS OF THE WEEK

Monday, it's the start of the week and I don't want to go to school.
I said, 'Daddy, please don't make me go in my class, I'm the fool!'
I always end up going and there I was standing at the door of
                                                  my classroom,
And hoping to go home *very, very* soon.

Tuesday, it's the second day of the week and closer to Friday.
In social education, no one ever wanted to hear my say!
In registration, everyone was jumping and having fun
And I was sitting in the corner reading my book on the sun!

Wednesday, it's the third day of the week and I'm all geared up
                                                  for netball.
In assembly, I was the only one listening in the whole hall!
In science I was the only one answering questions and to show
                                                  I was a geek,
I was the only one who knew every fact on the elections!

Thursday, it's the fourth day of the week and closer to the weekend.
The most popular girl actually talked to me, 'Would you have a
                                                  pen to lend?'
I was speechless and didn't know what to say,
I have to say that, that was the best day!

Friday, it's the fifth day of the week and the last day of school,
Some girls actually said to me, 'You can be cool!'
What would I say?
That this is the *best day!*

Shiza Khan (12)
Edgbaston High School For Girls

IS GOD REAL, I WONDER?

If God is all powerful,
Then why does he cause pain?
But is He the one who causes the pain?
Is He real? I wonder.

If He is all loving,
Then why does He not love all?
Why are there people who don't feel love,
Who do not feel His love?
Is He real? I wonder.

If evil exists, then does He exist?
Has He put evil in this world
To teach us good?
Has He created the evil to teach us bad?
Is He real? I wonder.

But my wondering has now ceased.
Is God real? I wondered.
Is He all powerful? I wondered.
Is He all loving? I wondered.
Does evil exist? I wondered.

How do I contemplate the answers?
I cannot find the answers by wondering,
I cannot find them by thinking,
I cannot find them by dreaming.

Is He real? I wondered, I thought, I dreamt.
No answers.

Parvinder Marwaha (16)
Edgbaston High School For Girls

THE SUN

As the morning grass is kissed by the morning dew,
Many people wake up to you.
You rise up over the horizon,
Animals awake at your call, none of which snore.

Sunshine graces each day
As children to go out to play.
Flowers bloom, leaves appear,
Now we know spring is here.

Bright, bouncing rays highlight each hour,
We feel your yellow, dancing power.
In the evening your rays are gold,
Under which stories are told.

How beautiful are your fingers of gold,
Here and now and in times of old,
Feeling your way into every house,
Driving darkness away forever.

You chase away dark winter months with
Your happy, delicate rays.
You shine throughout the day
And never go away.

As every hour has nearly gone
And evening is approaching,
You get ready to set.
Nobody can forget your golden-red ray,
That is used to light the way.

Becky Simm (12)
Edgbaston High School For Girls

LEPER

In a cave on the mountainside,
Overgrown, dark, damp, tired,
Old as old and cool as night,
This was the home of a man exiled.

A man whose face is peeling and raw,
Missing fingers and hidden toes,
Rotting flesh and matted hair,
Yet kindly eyes and helping hands.

He owns a bell he used to ring,
In the town he used to live.
It was there to warn of his coming in the street,
People drew back. Leper, leper.

He always tried to help the poor and begging,
But even they drew back in fear.
Disowned by his family, rejected by his friends,
Sent away, alone.

He arrived at the cave which was bare and cold,
But he learned to love it and make it alive.
He befriended the birds and cared for the land,
He saw the world was beautiful.

He still remembered the people,
But it didn't matter so much.
He knew something they didn't,
He knew how to love.

Hannah Parker (13)
Edgbaston High School For Girls

TIGER!

Tigers crawl across the ground
To pounce on their prey.
Their colourful camouflage will catch your eye,
Unlike any other creature passing by.

Oh how I wish I could ride on him,
Through the jungle and across snowy mountains.
His roar is scary,
But his fur is soft and fluffy.
His paws make massive prints
Which I sink into.

When bedtime comes I snuggle up to him,
Then he puts his paws around me and I feel so safe.
I dream of a time when we can fly above the sky
And sing and dance until the sun comes up.

As we wake, he makes a loud and scary yawn
Which makes me jump out of my skin,
And so I run and hide up a tree.
As he crouches down to pounce,
I see a tiny mouse,
I hear a whimpering squeak as the mouse is gobbled away.

As I climb down the tree, I feel his body against my leg,
So I pat him on the head
And cuddle him for a while.
I wish I could take him home and keep him forever.

Michél Ward (12)
Edgbaston High School For Girls

THE UNICORN

It was the ghost of an idea,
The glimmer of imagination,
The ice had been broken,
Mist became a shape,
Yet, still wandering aimlessly,
In the forest of our minds.

It began with the horn,
Shaped like an icicle.
From the horn came the head,
The eye like the universe,
Deep and dark with a twinkle of starlight,
An arch of a neck with dull, white lustre.

Flowing mane as if woven with air and water,
Gleaming hooves materialising
From the fog of our trees,
A glowing back that will never hold a saddle,
Swirling tail like strands of silver,
It stood, a gleaming pillar of pearly white and crystal.

It pricked its ears, listening,
It sniffed the air, checking for danger.
It stepped forward cautious, ever cautious,
Frosty grass crackled like thin ice,
Breeze blew the trees
And the unicorn began to eat.

Miriam Namih (13)
Edgbaston High School For Girls

HORSE SPIRIT

There it goes across the moor,
Its hair streaming like water,
Its silky, brown fur glistening
In the evening sun.
Its glossy mane stops flowing
As it slows to a gentle trot.

I wonder what it does all day,
As I watch it toss its head.
Maybe it canters across the moor,
Or maybe it just stands,
Watching the day go by,
Watching the sun go down.

But now I shall never know
What it does all day.
It once was wild and free,
Now it is tame and in bondage.
As I see its still silky, brown fur,
I also see the light gone from its eyes.

As it lays its restless head
Down for the last time,
I see its eyes drift to the moors,
I know its spirit is still there,
Even though its soul
Has now gone.

Mary Jack (13)
Edgbaston High School For Girls

WHAT DID I MISS?

In my carriage, I looked out of the window.
The Massai men floated past with garish, spotted blankets.
My eyes felt weary and suddenly I was asleep.
What did I miss?
If the train could talk,
What would it say?
Would it tell me of the plains of Africa dotted with acacia trees?
If the wind could listen,
What would it have heard?
The cries of the baboons when found by the leopards?
If the moon could touch,
What would it have touched?
The long neck of the giraffe or the dainty trotters of the warthog?
If the night could smell,
What would it have smelt?
Would it have smelt the rotting carcasses of dead animals?
If the grass could taste,
What would it have tasted?
Would it be mealie-meal that African families live on for years?
Did I miss the big, begging eyes of African children?
Did I miss them huddled together for warmth?
Did I miss seeing the poverty of some families?
Would I have felt lucky or sad?
What did I miss?

Philippa Lilford (12)
Edgbaston High School For Girls

EVIL

A man . . .
Walking barefoot in a river of blood.

He is naked . . .
The fire started by terrorists has burnt
The clothes off his back.

He has no feelings . . .
Numb with disbelief, he wades through
The lake of blood into the burning red sunset
To start again, alongside evil.

Rebecca Hobbs (15)
Edgbaston High School For Girls

PARADISE

The bare savannah with green, lush grass in patches,
The roaming wildebeest, the running zebras,
Their stripes clashing like swords.
A lonely warthog sniffing at the ground,
Is this paradise for animals?

But wait, is that a creeping lioness?
Ears pricking to the wind,
Paws lightly pressing the sand,
Her eyes straight ahead, peering at her prey.
Is this paradise for animals?

The limping zebra, lagging behind,
The others running on ahead,
Nobody notices it lying on the ground,
Breathing shallow, quick gasps of air.
Is this paradise for animals?

The lioness runs,
The zebra kicks,
Sand flying,
The bite fatal.
Is this paradise for animals?

Do animals have paradise?
We will never know!

Montserrat Thorp (12)
Edgbaston High School For Girls

HELP!

Help!
body in water
diving
cold
I want to go
nothing to save the body with, only me
snowing
car whizzing past
no one stopping

Help!
murky water
glass cutting through my foot
must carry on

Help!
can't see
my bones are cold
the body - dead?

Help!
got there
the body's cold
turn over
it's a man
heavy
swim
fog

Help!
side drawing nearer
silt covering him
I'll never get out of here

Help!

Louise Best (13)
Edgbaston High School For Girls

ROMANCE

Romance is like a flower, blossoming for a while and then dying.
Romance is like a cut, when someone breaks your heart,
You're scarred for life
Romance is like a page in a book, when someone leaves you
You turn the page over.
Romance is like a sentence, a few simple words and it's over.
Romance is like a song, you cherish the words forever.
Romance is like a river, you slowly drift apart
From the person you like most.
Romance is like a woodpecker, forever hammering at your heart.
Romance is like the sun, sometimes it shines, sometimes it doesn't.
Romance is like my heart, it's always there.

Emma Matts (12)
Edgbaston High School For Girls

SOFT PETALS

A burgundy rose
Placed on soft, moist snow,
Becoming extinct in the damp morning air,
Beads of dew trickle down its soft petals.
It's left to wilt,
The wind will play with it,
Slowly stripping it bare of its soft, fragile petals,
Leaving the stem to be cast into a fire of embers and smoke.
Scarlet and sunset yellows rise above it,
Leaving it as a small, grey mound of ash,
Drifting up through the darkness,
To the twilight air.

Charlotte Morby (13)
Edgbaston High School For Girls

BLACK FOREST

Dappled shade where lions creep,
Birds wide awake,
Or fast asleep.
Tall trees make a canopy overhead,
Brightly coloured butterflies, flashes of red.
Oh how I wish I could be there,
Small birds flitting through the air.
A fish through water doesn't make a sound,
A lion's roar will shake the ground.
The soft thud of a distant elephant's feet,
As I am walking, who or what might I meet?
Guava-green foliage brushes my face,
A leopard runs through the trees as if in a race.
I feel the soft petals of a passion flower,
As I sit by the water for hour on hour.
Eventually I have to go,
When I will return here, I do not know,
But I love the forest
And that's for sure.
Even the sky is a deep azure.
I love the wind,
I love the bees,
I love the soft green leaves.
I know I will be back some day,
If even in my dreams.

Alex Moorhouse (12)
Edgbaston High School For Girls

I AM...

I am the book you don't want to read,
I am the words you don't want to say,
I am the student you don't want to teach,
I am the air you don't want to breathe,
I am the scent you don't want to smell,
I am the song you don't want to sing,
I am the light you don't want to shine,
I am the fire you don't want to burn,
I am the path you don't want to follow,
I am the life you don't want to lead,
I am the goal you don't want to achieve,
I am the love you don't want to receive.

Kellianne Bartley (13)
Edgbaston High School For Girls

UNTITLED

Evil exists, that's what we believe,
I don't think God is there - to put it at ease.
You may go into church and put your hands together
And say God is all powerful for ever and ever.
But have you ever seen this powerful being?
The one who is all hearing and all seeing.
So explanations, we need some of those,
Start making a list of the cons and the pros,
Of having evil and the fact we're the predators,
Let's think about it now, instead of later.

Rachel Stacey & Katy Wright (13)
Edgbaston High School For Girls

THE ROSE

Murder, poverty, crime - God is love.
There's a rose, but the thorns pierce you.
A dark cloud emerges in my mind,
I can hear the thunder and the lightning,
But then I remember, the sun rises again.

Ignorance, fear, hate - God exists.
There's a rose, but the thorns turn inwards.
I feel painful emotions and scarring wounds,
But then I remember,
Wounds heal and emotions change.

Love, understanding, life - evil exists.
There's a rose and the thorns protect you.
Forever whole and complete,
You understand evil exists because
God is love and God exists.

Palvi Sahnam (15)
Edgbaston High School For Girls

RAINBOW FALLS!

Red is power and anger,
Orange is speed,
Yellow is ferocity and savagery,
Green is peacefulness and quietness,
Blue is lazy and calm,
Indigo is outgoing and is full of itself,
Violet is cheerfulness and happiness.

Beccy Newman (11)
Edgbaston High School For Girls

BLUE IS BLUEBELLS

Blue is:
Bluebells,
Bright, bouncy.

Sky,
Brilliant, breezy.

Ocean,
Beautiful, bewitched.

Swimming pool,
Balmy, bubbly.

Paint,
Background, blunder.

Rebecca Milford (12)
Edgbaston High School For Girls

LIFE

How can it be fun
When if you don't play well,
You lose your way?

When you wander
Off the trail
And things obscure your view.

Life is a game,
Play it well
And you'll win.

Alex Swartz (13)
Edgbaston High School For Girls

THE MAD SCIENTIST

Clang, bang, crash, boom,
The mad scientist will be out too soon,
Banging, crashing, smashing glass,
Oh no, there goes another. Arrrgh!
The mad scientist is back again,
Never will things be the same.

A big explosion on the way,
More and more booms every day,
Trying to get out of here,
Working non-stop without fear.
The mad scientist is back again,
Never will things be the same.

Charlotte Moxon (12)
Edgbaston High School For Girls

WAR

I know that I shall find my fate somewhere among the clouds,
The years that have gone seem a waste of breath,
A waste of breath, the years behind.

Those who I fight, I do not hate,
Those who are gone, I do not love,
This battle of Earth seems a waste of skin,
A waste of skin is this battle of Earth.

This weary attack seems all too much for my body,
My body is this weary attack.

The war ends and I am free,
Am I free or is this war an act of innocence?
An act of innocence is this weary war.

Alamin Siddique (13)
Golden Hillock School

GROOVY POEM

My name is Tabassum,
I am very tall,
But I never fall.
I am always shopping,
But I'm never stopping.
I am always smiling,
But I'm never crying.
I am very smart
And look after my heart.
I am usually nice,
I love chilli spice.
I'm mad about pop,
I love grooving.
When I go to a party,
I love moving.

Tabassum Bibi (11)
Golden Hillock School

SCHOOL: LESSONS AND TEACHERS

My name's Arfan,
His name's Yaser,
We hate school
Because the teachers think they're cool.
We hate lessons, they're so boring,
We start snoring.
We like cricket,
It's so wicked.
When we're doing work we can be lazy,
But we write something crazy.

Arfan Zafar (12)
Golden Hillock School

THE BEAUTIFUL GAME

The beautiful game,
The fantastic players,
I always dreamed about meeting footballers,
But I never met any of them,
To ask them what they think about football,
But never had a chance to ask them.
A sudden increase in travelling towards their goal.
Without stopping,
Is a dream of a young person.
I wish I could play football,
Be in the same football ground as them,
Get footballers' autographs,
Sit next to them,
Talk to them,
Even to play football with them if I get a chance to.

Mahpara Kanwal (13)
Golden Hillock School

SILENCE

S ilence
I ncessant insects scurry and scrape
L eaves laugh, tickled by the breeze
E verything is silent
N oisy streams trickle by
C louds are blown away by the wind
E verything is silent.

Kadija Yesmin (13)
Golden Hillock School

ATTACK ON NEW YORK

Remember, remember the eleventh of September,
The day New York was attacked,
The day Bin Laden hid,
The day Americans got angry and shocked.
Will America get revenge or not,
The question I am asking myself.
50,000 people dead!
Bin Laden wanted dead or alive!
People are scared for their lives.
Muslims all over the word are scared
That they are going to be murdered.
Bush and Blair upset, do they want revenge or not,
That's the question I am asking myself.

Ayaan Abdullahi (11)
Golden Hillock School

CHILD BRIDE

Sitting there wondering when he would appear,
Here or there. Where?
In her silver, glittering dress, shining like a star,
Wondering where you are.
If only you were there, you would be the one
To make her happy and fill the space in her heart.
With all your love, you would be able to comfort her
And keep her smiling and shining like a wonderful star in the sky.
Appearing like a star, sparkling through my eyes.

Sajida Begum (12)
Golden Hillock School

I AM AN ORPHAN

I am an orphan,
So lonely, so sad,
My parents are not found yet,
My heart aches, bad.
There are other normal kids with their families,
Passing by with a little dance,
If only I had a family,
If only I had a chance.
Here and there, kids to play with,
They seem happy,
But deep inside, we are crying,
Because we haven't got any family.
When I first found out
My parents were lost at sea,
I was so angry and confused,
It couldn't be.
I'm just dreaming
Of somebody to come,
So I can be part of the big world out there
And try to have lots of fun.
I'm jealous of other children,
Who go past me every day,
They skip, smile and run,
But I can't do that because I am an orphan.

Shapla Begum (11)
Golden Hillock School

PHOENIX

Volcanoes erupt when I screech,
My flames are red as a ripe peach.

Through the night I scatter my flames,
I glide and float over huge cranes.

Morning awakes when I give a loud yawn
And my work is done when it is dawn.

I rest in peace in the red-hot lava,
After one hundred years I will awake with the magma.

Aminur Rahman (12)
Golden Hillock School

UNANSWERED QUESTIONS

I remember when I found out about the war,
America against Afghanistan.
When they bombed America,
Do you think they did it for fun,
Or for will, dignity, mightiness and power?
The plane was swooping down and closer,
Then *boom!* They crashed into the Twin Towers.

Why did the Afghans do it?
Is it a game?
It's true Afghans are fighting for their country and religion,
Who do you want to win the battle?
Who do you think is going to win?
Are they spreading bloodshed for fun or for pride?
Do you think they are jeopardising themselves for nothing?
Why do you think all the Afghans are putting themselves
At risk for absolutely no reason?
Do you think they are threatening people for fun?

Will I die?
Will my friends die?
Who will survive?
Who will win the war?
Will it carry on forever?

Shak Shamol (11)
Golden Hillock School

THE CLASS OF MY LIFE

Butch who patronised,
Sally, whom it hurt.
I remember when I punched Kurt.
Rosie who teased,
Her mother was not pleased.
Owen the clown,
Now all he does is frown.
I remember how I used to think
About smoking at the skating rink.
Now I am old,
The gas bill is not paid,
Three-thirty at Aintree
Should get me paid.
All the people in my class
I threw across the heavily-dewed grass.
When I was born,
If I only knew
That I would be abused:
Because the second I was born, I was refused.

Saeed Hussain (13)
Golden Hillock School

IT WAS TIME FOR THE CHANGE OF MY LIFE

I just got shot in the backbone,
I was bristling and afraid,
I laid on my back, gave a long groan,
Under the tree, under the shade.

I waited for someone to help me,
No nurse had come with first aid kit,
I just lay there weeping for mercy,
I wished at the start I'd said, 'I quit.'

It was too late, cos there was no time,
I thought to myself, 'oh no, my wife!'
I told my gang to stop all the crime,
It was time for the change of my life.

Liaquat Ali (13)
Golden Hillock School

ALTON TOWERS

I remember saying 'No' to the Oblivion,
But there was no stopping me now.
My mum and dad forced me,
I had to go on it.
My heart was pounding with fear.
If my sister could go on it, so could I.
I went on it after all.
I sat in the seat, the man said 'Don't look down.'
I felt angry, I screamed all the way through.
Aaargh! I got my picture, my face looked pale.

I got some ice cream to cool me down,
I got strawberry flavour.
I was glad I was off that sick-making machine.
My ice cream melted, it dropped off my cone.
It was hot and sticky, just like me.
I got a cold drink instead.

All the rides were shutting,
I had to get off.
I was upset.
I was waiting all day to go on the giant helter-skelter.
We were in the car, me and my family,
I kept wishing we had a few more hours.
What a magical day!

Isabella Sheiybani Johnson (12)
Golden Hillock School

MUHAMMED AND ME!

His name is Umar,
His name is Muhammed,
We are eleven,
We're in Year 7.
I love football,
I do too,
He supports Liverpool,
He supports Man U.
Umar's into TV
And sitting on the settee,
I like films,
On DVD.
I hate snakes
Which make
Rattling noises,
They're always biting.
We love to play
On a sunny day.
I love good games
With funny names.
We both love cars
And Mars bars!
We like cartoons
And balloons.
I like burgers
And I hate murders.

Umar Muhammed Malik (11)
Golden Hillock School

DEATH

Lying there, pale as death,
The box he lay in meaningless to me.

The blood in his body,
Turning to slime but still.
No movement,
No speech.

People say he will never wake,
But I know he will, but hours later,
No movement,
No speech.

I sit on my chair as old as me,
Looking at the unexciting box, but still,
No movement,
No speech.

I hear hisses and buzzes,
But they don't hiss and buzz,
They say, 'He will never wake.'

But enough time has gone,
Enough blood has dried,
Enough tears have dropped,
Enough soil has been scattered,
But still,
No movement,
No speech.

Kamran Abass (13)
Golden Hillock School

WHO OR WHAT'S THERE?

I opened the curtains,
I thought it was a dream
Until I heard
That very loud scream.

The floorboards creaked,
The door banged shut,
Who or what was there?
I needed something to cuddle me up.

A gust of wind,
A shiver down my spine,
Who's there?
I know you want me for dinner time.

An unfamiliar shadow ran past me,
Then I got scared,
But then I noticed
A human head.

It hid behind the curtain,
A hand came out,
My hands started shaking,
All my teeth dropped out.

There laid a book
On his palm,
Half-opened,
Words spoke, 'Calm.'

'Calm, calm, little child,
It's only me, butler Fred.
I'll have you for supper
And drink your blood for tea.'

Rushia Begum (11)
Golden Hillock School

AN ALPHABET POEM

A is for Annie, who never tries to fight,
B is for Betty, who never is polite.
C is for Carol, who is very nice,
D is for Derek, who is always eating rice.
E is for Emily, who has a sniffy nose,
F is for Fred, who has smelly toes.
G is for Gary, who never stops his song,
H is for Harry, who is never wrong.
I is for Irene, who is very fast,
J is for John, who's always the last.
K is for Karen, who is very good,
L is for Leanne, who's always wearing her hood.
M is for Mandy, who never eats meat,
N is for Natalie, who always forgets to eat.
O is for Owen, who thinks he's the best,
P is for Paul, who never fails his test.
Q is for Quince, who breaks all his toys,
R is for Ruby, who runs after boys.
S is for Sophie, who is very pretty,
T is for Terry, who is very witty.
U is for Ursula, who never washes her face,
V is for Vicky, who's fastest in the race.
W is for Williams, who's got a big heart,
X is for Xena, who's at the top of the chart.
Y is for Yasmin, who's scared of her daddy,
Z is for Zoë, who is always ready.

You've just read an alphabet poem
And you've probably forgotten all you knew,
But if you are one of these people,
The poem is true!

Noor Yasin (11)
Golden Hillock School

I Hate

I hate to cry
Because we all have tears,
I hate to cry
Because we all have fears.
I hate tears
Because we all get fears.

I hate maths
Because it's hard.
I hate maths
Because I hate numbers.

I hate to fly
Because I'm scared of heights.
I hate to fly
Because I might die.

I like to play
Because it's fun,
So I come out
As the sun does.

Rubel Miah (13)
Golden Hillock School

Best Friends

She's always been there for me,
Listened to my problems
And told me everything's all right,
Because she's my best friend.

She's never ignored me,
Or told me to get lost.
She's never fought with me
Because she's my best friend.

Someone who makes you think about him every day, every night,
Someone who leaves sweet and sexy messages on the phone,
Someone who doesn't give up until he gets you,
Someone who admires you.

Someone who loves you till death!

Anum Mahmood (12)
Golden Hillock School

LOVE

The girl of my dreams
Is everywhere.
Over here and
Over there.

I think of her every day,
Even the day she went away.

When I think of her I start to cry,
If this is love, I ask, why?

Her soul is blessed by everything,
And I find her the sweetest thing.

So I ask the people in the world,
Is this love or just a word?
So help me know, to understand,
What is love?

M Qasim Rafiq (13)
Golden Hillock School

MY NAME POEM

Yo! My name is Magnaz.

I'm mad about pop,
I always achieve my targets,
I'm right at the top!
I've got good handwriting, which is
Level 5 (highest)
I love drinking Five Alive!
I am never useless,
Always handy,
I love eating lots of candy!
I love cuddly and adorable toys,
They're definitely better than the boys!
I'm excellent at sleeping,
And good at creeping!

Yo! My surname is Begum!

I'm called Clever Clogs,
Because I'm brainy,
My clothes are never stainy!
I'm eager to shop,
I love to hop!
I'm usually known as a gorgeous babe
Who always looks fab!
I'm usually hardworking,
And only sometimes talking!
I'm naughty sometimes,
But hey, that's me!

Magnaz Begum (11)
Golden Hillock School

The Night Noise

Whistling wind in the night
Gives me a chill and a fright.
The neighbour's dog is growling,
The midnight wolf is howling.

Tree branches tapping on the window,
Floorboards creaking below,
Cans outside are rattling on the floor,
Wind is knocking on the door.

The clock has just struck twelve,
My piggy bank has just fallen off its shelf.
I can't go to sleep, what shall I do?
My face has turned all pale and blue!

Zahed Hussain (12)
Golden Hillock School

Secret Crush

I have a secret crush . . .
Every time I see him walking down the street,
He has his hair gelled back, ever so neat.
Every time I see him it sends a shiver down my spine,
He has a lovely smile, every time.
He is lovely from his feet to his hands,
He's sure to have many admiring fans.
Every time I see him my eyes roll about,
Every time I want to speak to him, not a sound comes out.
One day, he's sure to ask me out.

Amy Flood (12)
Hillcrest School For Girls

WAR

Bang go the drums of war,
Mothers fleeing, children too,
Shrapnel flying everywhere.
The sight of blood makes me heave.
As I lie here thinking,
I wonder,
Why does this happen to me?
Why is war here?
Will I escape?
Will sunlight ever touch me?
Will I see my family?
I don't know, I'll just have to wait and see.
But why me?

Claire Kennedy (11)
Hillcrest School For Girls

PEACE

Peace is easy to say,
But it is not often kept.
Some terrorists think it's mere play,
It is said, but rarely meant.
Peace is often the cause for alarm,
But only when very untrue,
It can cause a great deal of harm,
I think that they are very cruel.
To blow up the Twin Towers,
Was far, far beyond me.
They are plotting throughout the hour,
They would laugh to hurt you or me.

Emily Bailey (11)
Hillcrest School For Girls

JOURNEYS

Some journeys are troublesome,
And some are unbelievable.
You never know what to expect from journeys.
Some are frightful
And some are painful.
You can't rely on them to be safe can you?
Journeys are popular
And you can travel by a lot of ways,
It can be either a car, bus or an aeroplane.
Some journeys are dramatic
And some unreal!
Journeys are everywhere and you can have a journey at any time
Because while I'm writing this . . .
I'm taking a journey to the land where journeys never end!

Sana Anwar (13)
Hillcrest School For Girls

DON'T TELL ME THAT I TALK TOO MUCH

Don't tell me that I talk too much!
Don't say it!
Don't you dare!
I only say important things,
Like why it's raining.
Where or when or how or why or what
Might happen here or there.
And why a thing is this or that
And who is bound to care?
So don't tell me I talk too much!
Don't say it!
Don't you dare!

Zoe Coules (12)
Hillcrest School For Girls

FOOD

Warm, succulent cookies,
Sliding out of the oven,
Warm, succulent cookies
Being baked by the dozen.
Cookies, cookies, oh so sweet,
More and more for me to eat.

Chips, chunky and large, never mind how big,
Sizzling in the fat,
Chips, chunky and large, never mind how big,
Want a whole load in my lap.
Chips, chips, sizzle, sizzle, sizzle,
Oh what a lovely smell.

Yellow, boiled, sour sweets,
Tingling up my spine,
Yellow, boiled, sour sweets,
How many more are mine?
Sour sweets all in one,
Soon they'll all be gone.

Hazardously knobbly,
Sliding in my mouth,
Hazardously knobbly,
Going down south,
Twiglets, Twiglets, long and thin,
How many more can I cram in?

Oval, green and wet,
Squishy in my mouth,
Oval, green and wet,
They'll come out down south.
Squishy, oval, green and wet,
How many more grapes can I get?

Round, big and small,
Still warm in the middle,
Round, big and small,
Icing melts in the middle.
Cakes, cakes, round and long,
Can I have another slice?

Elisha Huxtable (13)
Hillcrest School For Girls

PEACE ON EARTH

Bombs are dropping,
Towers are falling,
All around me, how can this be?
I can hear people calling,
Why is this, all that I see?

It hurts deep down inside
To know people are hurting,
I'd like to help them but I can't,
I see lots of people dispersing,
They run in every direction as they part.

I feel some of the loss they feel,
But not as much as they must.
I'd love to help, to try and heal,
Their lives have turned to dust.
I wish there was something I could do.

Why can't there be peace,
So we can take away the loss?
Just put the terrorists on a leash
And then we can all just doss.

Kimberley Mohammed (14)
Hillcrest School For Girls

FROM A TEEN'S POINT OF VIEW

Don't tell me I'm only fourteen years old,
I won't listen to you, I won't do as I'm told.
Don't tell me what to do,
You don't even know me,
I know me better than you
And I will stay out with my mates in the park
And I will stay out late, well after dark.
I will go out with boys you don't like
And it doesn't bother me,
So you can take a hike.
You can't put an old head on young shoulders,
But you wouldn't understand
Because you're a lot older.
So get off my back
And stop trying to be my friend,
You can't put things right,
So stop trying to make amends.
Don't tell me I'm only fourteen years old,
I won't listen to you, I won't do as I'm told.
I know I walk around with a chip on my shoulder,
But we'll understand each other when I'm a bit older,
But after all that I've said,
I never meant to hurt you.
Just remember this,
I'll always love you.

Rebekah Ward (14)
Hillcrest School For Girls

FRIENDS

Friends are people who are there for you,
When you are feeling down.
They look after you when you are sad
And hate it when you frown.

Friends are people who you can trust
And they can trust you too,
They'll always keep your secrets and
They'll always stick up for you.

Cheryl Crawford (12)
Hillcrest School For Girls

MY DREAM JOURNEY

I am going to Australia, my dream holiday.
I am going in one week.
I can't wait to be in the hot weather,
That is my dream holiday in Australia.

When I get to my sister's chalet, I will unpack,
Then I will visit my way around different parts of Australia.
It will be the most beautiful, clean place with
Lots of healthy plants and animals surrounding the island.
My dream is that, to be in Australia.

It will be hot, clean, and my sister's place will be nicely done,
Her children will be really nice.
Well the plane was going really fast,
My stomach turned really funny. I felt so sick.

After hours on the plane, it made me feel really uncomfortable.
The flight was very bumpy.
I arrived at my sister's chalet, the children were really mean.
The chalet was damp and the furniture broken. It was a dirty place.

The animals were very unhealthy, nobody looked after them,
The plants were not watered enough because of the heat.
My dream was a nightmare.
That was my dream holiday in Australia.

Sarah Isham (13)
Hillcrest School For Girls

THE JOURNEY OF LIFE

At the age of one,
My life had only just begun.

At the age of two,
I learnt a lot of new things I could do.

At the age of three,
I started at my nursery.

At the age of four,
I grew just a little more.

At the age of five,
For knowledge I did strive.

At the age of six,
The magician at my party did some amazing tricks.

At the age of seven,
I wanted to be at secondary school,
So I wished I was eleven.

At the age of eight,
On weekends I was allowed to stay up late.

At the age of nine,
My education was coming on just fine.

At the age of ten,
My mom and dad bought me a rabbit called Ben.

At the age of eleven,
My rabbit got ill and went to heaven.

At the age of twelve,
I started secondary school and in my homework I did delve.

At the age of thirteen,
My childhood almost seemed like a dream.

Sarah Bathgate (13)
Hillcrest School For Girls

SCARY

Poems can be silly,
Poems can be funny,
Poems can be full of tears
And make you feel like a dummy.
But here's a poem that's really scary,
So phone up your mum or Auntie Mary . . .

As you lie in your bed at night,
You will hear a noise that gives you a fright,
So you walk over to the door, boom, boom, bang, even more.
You hold your position, too scared to move,
Your parents appear, they hit the roof,
But they still look deep under the bed,
Then that's where you find your old dolly's head
With a popped-out mind . . .

And that was my scary poem,
But don't worry, it was only made-up.

Sophie Martin (11)
Hillcrest School For Girls

REACHING FOR MY LIGHT

My smile has faded recently,
Although I still have you,
We parted ways, went separately,
Yet still my heart is blue.
Your warming eyes and caring glance,
They still make me weak,
You never even gave me a chance
To laugh aloud or speak.
But now I've come to realise
My heart won't easily break,
And strong I will soon arise,
Although my heart may ache.
I am strong and I will try,
With all of my might,
And sometimes although I may cry,
Still I'll find the light.

Stacey Graham (14)
Hillcrest School For Girls

NIGHTMARE POEM

It was a dark, dark night,
On this dark, dark day,
Over the hills and far away,
The little devils came out to play.

They're bright red, like a funny joker,
And they have an evil face like a monster.
Watch out, this poem is gonna scare ya.

They travel the world like a Rover,
They stare out at you at night,
Watching you with their bright red, evil eyes.
Watch out, because you might be in for a surprise!

Tukyia Brown (14)
Hillcrest School For Girls

THE EARTH

I am the Earth,
Listen to my cry,
Why do you pollute me?
Please don't let me die.

The canal water you destroy each day,
The clean air you pollute each day,
They all belong to me and I'll help them to stay!

I am the Earth,
Listen to my cry,
Why do you hurt me?
Please don't let me die.

The green grass you trample on each day,
The smooth road you litter on each day,
They all belong to me and I will love them in my own little way!

I am the Earth,
Listen to my cry,
Why do you destroy me?
Please don't let me die.

Sonia Shukat (11)
Hillcrest School For Girls

I'D LOVE TO BE...

I'd love to be a fish in the sea,
So that I could swim
In the blue, dark-blue, deep dark-blue,
Cold and hot, hungry sea.

I'd love to be a cat,
To jump up high on the big, biggest,
Brown brick, tall, steep wall,
So I don't need to go through other people's gardens.

I'd love to be myself,
Because no one is more important than me in my own, special way.
Everyone is the same as everyone else.

Rooth Georgeson-Cartwright (11)
Hillcrest School For Girls

SWEET JAMAICA

Sweet birds sing to me every day,
Upon de beautiful beach of Montego Bay.
De water looks so calm,
It feels I can hold Jamaica in my palm.
The sweet smell of fresh fruit makes me feel like a yout.
De pickney, dem play so merrily and sing so cheerfully.
The trees blow so softly, day and night,
God bless for this beautiful sight.
The wonderful food that we eat
Makes me feel joyful and sweet.
De beautiful land dat me live,
Makes me feel Jamaica is the place to live.

Sherrelle Williams (12)
Hillcrest School For Girls

Autumn Night

Ten o'clock on a cold, dark autumn night,
Silence, but listen hard.
The wind whistles past the house,
It runs around and around.
Rain taps gently against the window,
It's relaxing, aren't you glad you're inside?
In your bed, snuggled up tight,
The hot water bottle gurgles as you move your feet.
The lightning shoots through the curtain,
It lights up all the dark corners.
Aren't you glad you're inside?
The crash, the boom, the thunder starts,
Shut your eyes, heart beats fast,
Gripping your duvet,
Aren't you glad you're inside?
Morning comes; storm passes, safe,
Aren't you glad you were inside?

Natalie Smith (12)
Hillcrest School For Girls

Just Me!

I am only a child, it's just me,
When I've got no one to play with sometimes I get lonely.
I wish I had a sister,
So we could have lots of fun together.
We could stay up talking all night,
Until the sun shines clear and bright.
But I am only a child, it's just me.

Roxanne Conway (12)
Hillcrest School For Girls

THE FEELING

Love is the binder of the universe,
The glue of all mankind,
It is the key to a successful relationship,
That, as well as trust.
Belief in one another is the road to each other,
Without love,
Life isn't worth living,
Isn't worth living at all.
Like a field with no flowers,
Empty,
Plain,
Lifeless.
As helpful as this feeling can be,
It has its complications,
But like everything else when you experience this,
When you experience this overwhelming sensation,
All things are cleared from your mind.
Apart from your love provider, that is.
You know if you are in love,
The feeling is unique.
Permanently daydreaming,
Away you go,
Your head in the clouds.
Then back to Earth when you feel the tingling up your spine.
Amazing,
Unexplainable,
Perfect.
Love is the binder of the universe,
The glue of all mankind . . .

Samantha Cox (13)
Hillcrest School For Girls

I Love You

There he is,
Waiting for me,
Standing there
By the weeping willow tree.
When I went over,
He smiled so sweetly,
My heart beat very fast,
I came over all tingly.
He took my hand,
I took his too,
I looked in his eyes,
They stuck like glue.
I hadn't noticed his amazing eyes,
They were a wonderful blue,
They looked like the sea, washing on the sand.
He said while he took my other hand,
'I love you.'
The very next day, I met him again
By the same weeping willow.
He said, 'I love you.'
It took my strength, my courage and strain,
To realise what he had said again.
Again I met him by the weeping willow,
'I love you,' he said.
'I love you too,' I said, going quite red.
He smiled for at last I had said those worlds,
Then we kissed.
It wasn't so bad,
For I knew I had the best boyfriend
A girl could ever have!

Kimberley Dawes (12)
Hillcrest School For Girls

ANGER AFTER

I let it happen,
I knew it was wrong.
Anger, heat, bubbling inside me,
I stalked off
My friends talked to me, 'It's only stuff.'
I didn't do it, but it was all wrong,
The heat went; calmed down, my anger gone
There was an annoying thing itching in me,
A bubble about to pop.
It was screaming inside me,
Telling me to tell them to stop.
They want to go to the shop again.
I'd just about had enough,
I try and tell them to stop,
The scream inside won't calm down,
I feel dirty, angry and hot.
'It's only stuff,' they say again.
I lose it, I'm screaming, 'Stop, just stop.'
Shoplifting's wrong, it's morally wrong.
I was so angry, the only thing I could yell was, 'Stop!'

Catherine Brinsdon (13)
Hillcrest School For Girls

WIND IN THE WILLOWS

Wind in the willows,
Wind in the trees,
Wind rushing past and
Creating cool breeze.

Rippling over water,
Diamond-white light,
Whistling over treetops,
All through the night.

Wind in the willows,
Wind in the trees,
Wind rushing past and
Creating cool breeze.

Hannah Paddock (16)
Hillcrest School For Girls

SURPRISE JOURNEY

I am on a journey,
I don't know where to.
My mom said it was a surprise,
It's like being kidnapped,
I don't know where I am going.

I hope we are going somewhere fun.
'Mom, are we there yet?
Are we there yet?'
My mom said nothing.

My mom is playing her
Fogey's song on the radio.
I am so bored!
'Are we there yet?'

I am water, I never know where I am going,
I just go with the flow.
'Are we there yet?'
My mom said, 'Nearly.'

I am so excited,
I can't wait to get there,
'We're here.'
'Oh Mom, not the supermarket!
When are we going home?'

Charlotte Hathaway (13)
Hillcrest School For Girls

FRIENDSHIPS

Some people treat it like a joke,
They're your friend one minute and the next you're gone.
They treat you like a bottle of Coke,
Drain your fun out, then when you're last week's news
They throw you away.
Others use blackmail.
'If you give me your money, I'll be your best friend.'
They treat you like dirt, but you still hang on.
You think, maybe she'll change, just maybe,
She'll see me for who I really am.
Some people think it's funny to watch you being bullied,
They just stand in the background and watch.
You think, 'If they're my friends, then why aren't they helping me?'
Then fear kicks in, 'If I'm mad at them, they won't be my friends.'
Decent people think of it as gold,
They treasure, worship and hope it will always be.
Friendship is a fickle thing.
How do you treat it?

Natalie Mercier (12)
Hillcrest School For Girls

THE BLUE SKY

I look at the sky
So nice and blue,
It shines so bright into my eyes.
The colour of sky blue is nice in the sky,
It hits you nice and soft.
The colour is like my blue pen, but nice and smooth,
Soft and smooth,
Not hard, only when it becomes night.

When the clouds come out
It starts to rain,
The sky goes dark,
So dark and hard.
When the morning comes
The lovely sky is sky blue,
So smooth and soft.

Ashia Hamid (12)
Hillcrest School For Girls

TILL DEATH DO US PART

From the hospital room
To the classroom,
Life goes on.
To the first 'A',
To the first 'D',
Life goes on.
From the first date
To the first child,
Life always goes on.
I was a baby,
You were a baby,
Life has gone on, because we're already years on.
From the first breath of air
To the last breath of air,
That's when life doesn't go on.
You might go to hell,
You might go to heaven,
But this only happens
When death do us part.

Fayola Lezama (14)
Hillcrest School For Girls

THE BEGINNING

As he stood and stared at me passionately,
I felt a chill run down my spine;
I felt young again.
As he looked into my eyes,
I saw a deep, loving side of him;
I saw love, in capital letters.
As he whispered in my ear,
I felt warmth go through my body,
I felt my fingertips tingle.
As he put his arms around me,
I felt unreal, but warm,
I felt right.
As he kissed me softly,
I felt a numbness in my lips,
I felt like a whole new start had begun.

Nicola Strolin (14)
Hillcrest School For Girls

LOVE IS...

Love is the colour of pink,
Love tastes like candyfloss,
Love feels like fluffy, yellow chicks,
Love looks like a bunch of roses.

Love is an angel sent down from heaven,
Love tastes like melted chocolate,
Love feels like fluffy clouds in the sky,
Love looks like your favourite pop star.

Love is you!

Lyndsey Smith (12)
Hillcrest School For Girls

LOST

Wandering through the rain,
Cold and damp,
I can't believe he left me,
Left me to walk in the rain.
Droplets hit like daggers,
Can't blame them,
It's the pain that hits.
Not the droplets.
Cold sinks deeper into my heart,
He left me,
Cold on the outside,
Saturated,
Rain or tears?
Cold on the inside,
Saturated,
Pain and dejection.
He left me,
Here, in the rain.
I can't believe he left me.
Depression hits,
Sweeps over me like a blanket of cold.
What did I do wrong?
The rain beats still harder,
Lashing at my crying soul.
I walk further on.
But suddenly, the rain slows, stops,
The sun peeps out from behind a cloud.
Its rays penetrate my cold skin,
Warming, soothing
And there he is,
Standing like an angel,
Like a dream.
'I'm sorry,' he says.

Stacey Frost (16)
Hillcrest School For Girls

BOOKS THAT I READ

On Monday, I read in a butcher's shop
And as I was reading, I heard chop, chop, chop.

On Tuesday, I read in a market place
And as I was reading, I saw girls selling lace.

On Wednesday I read in a cinema
And as I was reading, I heard the beep of a car.

On Thursday, I read in a shopping mall
And as I was reading, there were men posing tall.

On Friday, I read in a little friend's house
And as I was reading, I heard the squeak of a mouse.

On Saturday, I read inside a church
And as I was reading, I saw a little dove perch.

On Sunday, I was tucked into my bed,
Thinking of all the books I had read.

Jolande Allen (12)
Hillcrest School For Girls

MY TRIP TO NEW YORK
(In loving memory to all those who suffered in this tragedy)

Oh my gosh!
I'm going to New York.
It's a dream come true,
Only one more week to go!

I said goodbye to my family,
'See you in two weeks time.'
I'm going to miss them,
But I'll see them soon.

As I took off,
I felt light as a feather.
I couldn't believe it,
I was going to New York.

I was on the plane for nine hours,
Then the captain shouted,
'We're going to crash into the two big towers,'
Silence.

Nicola Minks (14)
Hillcrest School For Girls

MY PET DOG

My pet dog makes such a mess,
Why, oh why does my dog make such a mess?

He barks so loudly and wakes up all the neighbours,
Why, oh why does he bark so loudly and wake up all the neighbours?

My pet dog bites my pink skirt,
Why, oh why does my dog bite my pink skirt?

He bites the Sunday paper when it's just been bought,
Why, oh why does he bite the Sunday paper when it's just been bought?

My pet dog licks my face,
Why, oh why does my pet dog lick my face?

He pulls my dolls' heads out of their bodies,
Why, oh why does he pull my dolls' heads out of their bodies?

My pet dog annoys me sometimes,
Why, oh why does my pet dog annoy me sometimes?

Because he's a dog and that's what dogs do!

Laura Carty (12)
Hillcrest School For Girls

CHOCOLATE, CHOCOLATE

Chocolate, chocolate,
It's all I think about,
Chocolate, chocolate,
I love it without a doubt.

Chocolate, chocolate,
I'll eat any kind,
Chocolate, chocolate,
It's always on my mind.

Chocolate, chocolate,
Melting on your tongue,
Chocolate, chocolate,
Eating it's so much fun.

Kaisha Campbell (12)
Hillcrest School For Girls

A JOURNEY TO MY DREAM

How I wish I could touch the sky,
How I wish I'd never had to say goodbye,
How I wish I could eat food
That would put me in a very good mood.
How I wish that I wasn't rude,
Oh why do people think I'm a prude?
Just a few wishes could make things better.

Dannielle Caudy (13)
Hillcrest School For Girls

NIGHTMARE POEM

It was a dark, cold night,
No one was about,
Everything was quiet,
There was only me that was out.

So I walked along the park
And it was very dark.
Then all of a sudden,
I saw a bright yellow spark.

So I looked all around,
Still nothing, not a sound.
The little spark got bigger,
In the darkness was a tall, dark figure.

The figure was drawing near,
It was the biggest, scariest fear.
I got up and ran as fast as I could,
Through stones, rocks and mud.

Never once did I look behind,
It was so dark, I felt as if I was blind.
I reached my house, ran through the door,
Then I curled up in a tight little ball.

I had never felt so much fright
As on that dark, cold night.

Amie Herbert (14)
Hillcrest School For Girls

THE MALL

Screaming, screaming, that's all I hear,
Pick me, come to me, have no fear!
One floor, three floors, I'm losing count,
How much money should I take out?
£5, £10, 15, £20 - £5, £10, £15, £20?
Around, around in my head,
That's all I think about until I am fed!

This one, that one, I'm going in here,
No you're not, says my conscious fear.
I'm arguing, wrestling with my fear,
No one around me, no one can hear.
So many words all here at once,
I bet they've been here for the last five months.

That's it, I'm there, I'm going in.
I've just been in a shop called LIN.
I'm bored, let's go, I want to go back,
But there he is, my friend called Mac.
I tell him my troubles, but he's in a mood,
So I don't bother going to order my food.

My friend's in a mood,
My fear's a pain,
This is seriously driving me insane.
I love the mall, I love it, I love it.
Screaming, screaming in my head,
Pick me, come to me, that's all they said.
I'm big, I'm long and very, very tall,
I'm the one, the only, the great, great mall!

Caroline Dunnett (13)
Hillcrest School For Girls

THE CHILL OF AUTUMN

The cracking of the chestnuts,
The crick of the cricket,
The howling of the wind,
The prowling of the wolves.

The roar of the fire,
If you go out now,
The consequences
Will be dire.

The witching hour,
Under the bed sheets you'll cower.
The full moon lights up
The place of your doom.

The leaves falling,
The spirits calling,
The fireworks blazing,
The flashes and booms dazing,
The dogs growling.

The water falling,
The knife mauling,
Those soul-searching eyes,
The heart-stopping cries.

The branches whip and scratch your face,
Your heart and your legs having a race,
And then you stop,
Dead!

Anna-Marie Averill (12)
Hillcrest School For Girls

THE JAGUAR

Wandering around
The winding wilderness,
Staring into clean cages.
The apes chattered
And swung around in the sun,
Safe and secure from the hunter's gun.

Parrots, splotched with all
The colours of the rainbow,
Strutted and squawked.
Gleaming feathers
Were well looked after.

Excited with activity,
Tigers and lions
Raced as fast as lightning,
Entertaining the pushing and shoving crowd.
Children's faces gleamed with excitement.

In the last cage,
A shiny, jet-black jaguar
Lay lazily in the sun,
Moving a massive paw
Over its contented face.

Sleek muscles moved
Under its taught fur,
As it meandered over to the bars,
Interest shone in its red eyes,
Then it turned and went back
To its patch in the sun.

Emma Savage (15)
Hillcrest School For Girls

MY LOVE FOR YOU

Since the first time I saw you, I have loved you.
My love for you is eternal,
It is like a waterfall,
Showering more and more love on to you,
For you mean everything to me,
More than you can comprehend.

I try to show you, but how can I?
You're not here with me,
You can't love an image in your head
Or a photo on your wall.
I hope that one day . . . just one day
I'll see you, see you in my college,

Smiling at me.

I know these fantasies won't come true,
But I can still dream.

My love for you is like
An alcoholic's love of beer,
As they can't live without it,
I can't live without you.

I hope we stay together, because you're my all
And I never want to be without you,
Even though every day I feel I am.
I love you,
And the question is,
Do you love me too?

Rosie Tearle (15)
Hillcrest School For Girls

AUTUMN SO BRIGHT

An ancient-looking figure
Stood in a field,
Looked like a scarecrow,
Felt like a ghost.
He stood there whistling,
Like the morning wind,
Looked like a scarecrow,
Felt like a ghost.
He wore a long cloak
Made of bright leaves.
Looked like a scarecrow,
Felt like a ghost.
He was no scarecrow,
He was just autumn.
Autumn so light,
Autumn so bright.

Faye Burrows (13)
Hillcrest School For Girls

SHE STOOD

She stood in her home
Watching the plane,
It hit the World Trade Center.
She screamed,
She ran out into the street.
There was a child in the pram,
She picked the child up and said,
'Why?'

She fell to the ground
And watched it crumble.
She ran into her home,
She sat and stared,
Holding the child close,
And sat and sang.

Cressida McDonnell (13)
Hillcrest School For Girls

THIS IS WAR

I sit and watch the sun set,
I can see all the soldiers' silhouettes,
With their guns at rest upon their chests,
They wait and wait for their time to come,
For they will never know
When their enemies decide to play and have fun.
Well, that's what it seems,
As though they like to kill and hurt each other.
I hate it, as so would all their mothers.
Their own baby boys out there protecting their religion.
In despair, they fight, kill and kick,
Whilst I can only watch and feel so ill and sick,
And then, for a small while,
Everywhere is still and quiet,
Until it starts all again, with arguments,
Guns and yet more and more pain.
As I sit and watch the sun set,
I can see all the soldiers silhouettes.

Keeley Murray (13)
Holy Trinity RC School

SORROW, ANGER AND HATRED

The soldiers through the valley walk,
They look to their left,
And to their right.
There are some other soldiers in sight.

They reach for their guns
And their grenades,
They've already been fighting for days,
But somehow they carry on.

Keep on fighting to the rise of the sun,
Many lives are lost,
Many minds are blown,
Many souls are gone,
Never going home.

Sorrow, anger, hatred and war,
Burning fire,
Nowhere to retire,
But they have to fight
For their right
To live life.

Coan Gayle (13)
Holy Trinity RC School

IRELAND'S NOT IRELAND ANYMORE

Ireland is not Ireland anymore,
The happiness has gone,
It's now Ireland at war.
People are crying.
Soldiers are dying.
And I'm still lying here in my bed.

Blood is running, running like water,
Soldiers are sent out like cows to the slaughter.
I'm just a little girl, I was someone's daughter,
But now my father's dead
And I'm still crying, lying here in my bed.
Ireland's not Ireland anymore.

Amelia Asquith (13)
Holy Trinity RC School

BEAUTIFUL LAND

I don't want to fight any more
Please take me out of this terrible war,
Kill me, hurt me, shoot me dead,
Because I'm sick and tired of seeing the blood run red.

I'm sick and tired of hearing the bloodcurdling screams,
The bloodcurdling screams of fellow human beings,
I just want to know why we are fighting,
Why we are killing, crying and dying.

Why are we blowing up this beautiful land,
Turning this world into dust and sand?
Let's just stop the war now, for no one will win,
By continuing this war we are committing a sin.

Why can't someone just stop this war,
So peace can settle over the land like before.
God, please give us a Martin Luther King
So he can bring peace,
So we can all laugh and sing.

Ashley Newell (13)
Holy Trinity RC School

A Poem Of War

I watch the violence as though it were a parade of fireworks,
Dazzling but dangerous.
I hear the pain as though it were a baby's cry
For attention and love.
The constant fight of injustice,
The enemy invisible,
Nobody knows when their time is up,
Many waiting, the time unbearable.

War is like a volcano, it could erupt anytime,
The innocent dying first.
The deaths are counted like birds
Flying through the open blue sky,
All the people killed having families,
Nobody thinks though,
Nobody cares who dies.

Many scared it could be a loved one,
The slight chance a child.
People wondering what if?
The sudden spurt of maturity in the young,
All mothers wanting to protect,
War just like a game,
You get caught and you're out.

Laura Douglas (13)
Holy Trinity RC School

Freedom

All people should be treated equally and be free,
Not locked away like prisoners.
They should have the right to say what they think,
Speak freely, without being punished or beaten.

To be treated how others would like to be treated
And not be judged because their skin colour is different.
After all, there is only one race,
The human race.

Nathan Burrell (12)
Holy Trinity RC School

BUT I AM DEAD

Bombs are flying,
People are dying,
Soldiers are crying,
But I just stare.

Guns are gunning,
People are running,
Soldiers are coming,
But I'm unaware.

Bombs are exploding,
Guns are unloading,
Soldiers are moaning,
But I don't care.

Bombs are beeping,
People are weeping,
Soldiers are creeping,
But I rest my head.

Bombs are flying,
People are dying,
Soldiers are crying,
But I am dead.

Jerome Hall (13)
Holy Trinity RC School

WAR

People are crying,
People are dying,
Victims, fallen, breathing their last breath,
Thinking, when will we come back to carry on our life?
Thinking about the people we are leaving behind,
Shouting out, 'Help,'
And no one coming,
Too busy killing,
Never knowing when it will all stop,
Thinking, why did we ever get involved?
Thinking, we are the innocent ones, don't kill us.
Shouting out 'Help!' again and no one coming,
Acting as if nothing is happening.

Ammar Choudhry (13)
Holy Trinity RC School

AT WAR

Bang, bang go the guns, shouting really loud,
They have hit the target they finally found.

The target they hit screamed really loud,
They got them back and they screamed really loud.

The people who were watching got really scared
And took their families where they would not be heard.

The children were scared, the parents were scared,
But all they could do was to keep well away from them.

Bang, bang go the guns once again.

Chantelle Frue (14)
Holy Trinity RC School

WAR

Bang, bang, bang, the bombs land,
Flying through the air and onto the ground.
Every day you see them fly.
Then you see people die
From the shootings every night,
They give you such a fright.

All day I wait to see
What is going to become of me.
Will I die, or will I live?
To see it people will give
A bit of mercy instead of this,
Bombing our towns and cities all night.

When we wake up in the morning,
The devastation that I see
Really saddens me,
With all the houses
That have been blown up
By the bombs of the enemy.

The invisible enemy
That we cannot see,
They could be lurking, waiting for me.
Shooting, firing with their guns,
It could be our mates, or our mums.

The guns are firing,
Killing innocent people
Who are asleep.
Everybody's crying for their loved ones.
War is bad and war should stop.

Daniel Gallagher (13)
Holy Trinity RC School

STREET WAR

You can hear the bombs from down the street,
People getting blown up from head to feet.
When you see all this pain,
It is enough to drive anyone insane,
But what can you do?
It's something no one can get used to,
The years go by and every night I cry
And wonder when is it my turn to die?

You look around and what do you see?
Blood that flows indiscriminately.

I used to be scared of dying in my heat and mind,
But now I would just really love to leave this world behind.

No one cares about people and me,
They just care about victory
And when I die,
In my bed I hope to lie, and
For the nation to be a friend
And for this terrible war to end.

Kayleigh Burns (13)
Holy Trinity RC School

WHEN WILL THIS STOP?

Bombs coming out of the sky
And innocent people die.

People of the city crying for help,
But there is no stopping of the bombs coming down.

Gun noises everywhere, can't get any sleep,
When will they stop, for peace?

Blood on the grass, blood on the floor
And when will they stop this killing war?

Anil Singh (13)
Holy Trinity RC School

GOALS

As we watch, freezing in a T-shirt,
Hold our scarves high,
Our heroes walking down the tunnel,
A sea of blue and white.
When you glare to the right, you see the cup,
You wonder if it's your year this year.
At half-time, the rush for the toilet.
Eventually, the last minute came,
Ball played over the top,
It's controlled,
It's a goal!
Could we really win the cup?
Up, up, the crowd rise,
It feels like forever.
We all whistle nervously,
And then,
Whooo, whooo, whooo!
We've won!
The captain lifts the cup,
What a difference a goal makes!

John McDougall (13)
Holy Trinity RC School

GOODBYE

This is a world of terrorism,
Where my little boy is included.
Bombing, missiles and petrol bombs,
While my little boy is missing.

Attack, pain and terror,
But still no sign of my boy.
Violence, threatened and endangered is my little son,
Waiting for his mother's coming.

Conflict, traumatic and ugly,
The world is becoming
Heartless, scared and worried is the loving mother,
But still no sign of my little boy.

Heartbroken and scared is my little boy,
Searching for his loving mother.
Attack, violence and war starts again,
Where is my little boy?

Tasmira Ahmed (13)
Holy Trinity RC School

WAR POEM

There is a violent enemy,
Where lives are on hold,
Not knowing when the next strike will be,
Not knowing who is our enemy.

Fear rises up in each and every one of us,
It takes hold of our being,
Like our shadow,
It is always there, never ending.

When will peace come to the world?
When will everyone be happy like never before?
We are all brothers and sisters in God's family,
There is no justice in war.

Karolis Tertelis (13)
Holy Trinity RC School

AN ONGOING BATTLE

This is war,
I see the violence and attacks,
Disturbing images.
Divisions of people in an unsettled world.
Tragic are the circumstances.

The rage of the gun,
The ferocious flames that engulf their victim;
I fear the enemy whose anger knows no bounds,
He who is the aggressor,
The one who awaits the innocents' fall.

No choice between life and death,
Or when that invisible enemy strikes.
The next minutes seem bleak,
No longer is there the march of feet,
But only the faint beat of the ones left to weep.

If this war should ever end,
These families will never see their loved ones again,
For this is war,
An ongoing battle,
Where no one will be the victor in the end.

Sarah Lynch (13)
Holy Trinity RC School

FREEDOM

Freedom is bigger than anything,
It cannot be measured or compared,
Not to the vastness of the sea,
Not even to the infinity of space.
Freedom is what we make it.

What is freedom?
Freedom has many definitions to many people.
For some people freedom is a dream,
For others it's a reality.
For most of us, freedom is what we make.

Freedom to me is being able to
Make my own choices
Without pressure,
That is truly freedom.

Freedom to you is being able to
Do your own thing,
Being able to wander endlessly,
Freedom is what you make it.

Jamie Smith (12)
Holy Trinity RC School

FREEDOM

Freedom is like a key to life,
To have the independence to
Do things that you want to do,
To have an existence.

Being free is being you,
To have the opportunity,
The way of living,
To have liberty.

Take freedom wisely and be glad
To have the privilege,
Take note that not all people have freedom,
It's your advantage.

Freedom is your key to life,
Your latitude.
Be sensible with it,
Don't have 'attitude'!

Lauren Caballero (13)
Holy Trinity RC School

WAR

Someone please stop this war,
I don't want to see death any more.
The war has just begun,
Bullet vs bullet, gun vs gun.

Soldier after soldier awaits his fate,
All around is pain and hate,
Lifeless bodies scattered on the ground,
Mothers' precious sons that will never be found.

The soldiers await their death,
Taking their last breath,
All hope of peace is gone,
Soldier after soldier staring down the barrel of a gun.

Bang! A pull of a trigger, he is no more,
You look up and see violence and gore.
Why? All because of this stupid war.

Amina Khan (13)
Holy Trinity RC School

FREEDOM

Here I am, sitting in my room,
Wondering where I'm gonna go today.
I walk down the street, girls go out to play.
When I get on my bus, I sit down and look around,
There are people who go to work, they have their freedom.
I sit back and think, and say to myself, 'I have freedom.'

A bird that flies high in the sky,
With its wings spread out,
The wind blowing under his wings,
He has no worries at all.
I think to myself, 'He has freedom.'

Animals in the wild that run around,
The monkeys climb trees,
The bears sit down
And the lions look for their prey.
They have freedom.

John Claffey (12)
Holy Trinity RC School

FREEDOM

Having freedom is being able to express how you feel,
No one to tell you, express yourself.
Having freedom is doing what you want to do in your own time,
No one to tell you how to plan your day.
It's your choice what you want to do.
Having freedom is having opportunities that you pick,
No one to tell you how they feel about your choice.
Having freedom is have confidence and not feeling down when
                                        someone's around.

Just be yourself.
Having freedom is like building a new you, being a new person.
Having freedom isn't as much fun as you think.
Even when you're older, you say you don't need anyone,
You can control your own life,
But believe me, it's not true.
You always need people to be there for you.
Just remember, having freedom is fun, but don't take it for granted.
That's what freedom means to me.

Micheala McCalla (12)
Holy Trinity RC School

THIS IS WAR!

Death is coming, people take a breath and hope it's not their last,
The innocent are the ones crying out in pain,
Blood in puddles on the floor,
This is war!

The violence happening includes the invisible enemy we do not know.
The risk is taken to save the children of our time,
Trying to reunite the families that have been divided by the end
                                                             of the night.
This is war!

Terrorists attack, not knowing when it will happen again,
People, children, fear for their lives.
Tears fall like rain on the ones who are already suffering.
Hatred is what they are feeling.
This is war!

Emma White (13)
Holy Trinity RC School

FREEDOM

Freedom is to be able to make your own choices,
Freedom is when people hear your voice,
Freedom is to be your own boss,
If you don't have freedom, it's a terrible loss.

Freedom is to be free,
People without it should stop and think,
'What's happening to me?'

Everyone should be free,
Then it's a time to smile with glee.

We should live our own lives.
The world should have free girls and guys.

James Cotter
Holy Trinity RC School

FREEDOM

If there is no freedom,
There's no life.
You can't live without freedom.
Having freedom means to be able to make decisions,
You should not be owned by anyone,
Or have to do as they say.
Freedom is all about being free,
Not having to do as you are told to do.
No one should be in charge of you,
There is no point living without freedom,
It is better to die than not have freedom.

Faisal Ahmed
Holy Trinity RC School

FREEDOM

I was stuck in a shed,
I wanted to be free.
I locked myself in, but I lost the key.
I was banging, but nobody came,
I thought, help me, help me,
Am I to blame?

I was hungry and sleepy,
I was dead to the world.
I couldn't go to sleep in case somebody might come,
Maybe to let me out, or hide a gun.
If they hide a gun, I could shoot through the door,
Then I would get out and I wouldn't be in the shed anymore.

Think, think, how to get out?
Maybe I could shout.
Someone will hear me, that's my plan,
I wish I had my mobile and I could call Gran.
She lives across the road, she could come and get me.
Oh, I hope she will let me stay,
Because it is a horrible day.

Someone is coming, I'd better hide,
It could be a man, or could it be Gran?
I'll peep through the hole. Hey, it's Gran,
No it isn't, it is a man. 'Oh please let me out,
It's me, it's your favourite scout.'
'Oh there you are, we've been looking for you,
we couldn't even find a clue.
Go on, go on, run away as fast as you can
And don't come back another day.'

Sarah-Jane Williams (12)
Holy Trinity RC School

FREEDOM (MY MEANING)

A bird is so free
Out in the wild,
You can't say the same
For a little child.

When you're at home
And feeling so small,
You wait for your freedom
When you are tall.

When you grow up,
You are so free,
Travel the world
And like what you see.

Now you are older,
You'll have no fear.
Look all around you,
Your freedom is here.

Alex Walters (12)
Holy Trinity RC School

FREEDOM

Freedom is to leave everything behind,
To go into your own world.
Don't do what they tell you,
To make your own decisions.
Make up your own mind, be free!
Run away from all your troubles,
Let everyone come after you.
Freedom is to do your own thing.

No one is stopping you from having your dream.
So go, now is your chance to be free,
Run wild, do what you like.
Do something with your life.
Think over your problems.
Freedom is to go outside and play,
Just drift away . . .

Lyndsey Johnson
Holy Trinity RC School

FREEDOM

Finally, at last I am free,
Like an animal, a bird or a bee.
Finally, I can make it on my own,
With no restrictions in my home.

With no restraints in my life,
I could even have my own wife.
Because they are my own plans,
The fate of myself is in my own hands.

I could be king of the world,
With loads of diamonds and pearls.
I could have loads of cars
And live amongst the stars.

Freedom moves at its own pace,
With no limits, because life is no race.
You can move around in space,
You could become an artist, or just trace,
But anyway you put it, it's your plan,
Because the fate of your life's in your hands.

Joseph Barnett (12)
Holy Trinity RC School

TORTURE OF LOVE

Watching time fly by,
Miserably days go by,
Thinking about words you said,
Sitting up in my bed.

Dreaming of hearing your voice 24/7,
Already feeling like I'm in heaven.

Tossing and turning, endless sleep,
The sensual distraction the cause of heat,
Wanting to be with only you,
I hope you feel the same way too.

Ringing and bugging you,
I know you hate it, I know you do,
The sweet things that you say,
Guess you're used to saying them anyway.

'Absence makes the heart grow fonder,'
My love for you is getting stronger.
You're the key to my heart,
So please, don't tear my love apart.

Saima Sarwar (17)
Josiah Mason Sixth Form College

WHO MAKES THE RULES?

Someone must . . .
Who decided we should evolve?
Who decided kids are immature?
Who's the one who makes the rules?
Is it the one who creates us, or takes us?

If it's the one who creates us,
Why create us with boundaries?
If it's the one who takes us, why
Make rules to end us?
Who decides?

Melissa George (16)
Josiah Mason Sixth Form College

WOLF

Wolf.
Wild, wintry wolf,
That's what I am.
Softly I pad
Through a white, whirling world.
Rough, tough trees,
Green, mean leaves,
They poke through my coat.
Frost freezes everything,
She misses nothing.
Icicles are everywhere,
Cold, clear, cruel icicles.
The cold creeps in,
Here and there.
There is nothing anywhere,
Only me,
Walking through my own iced-over world.
Wild, wintry wolf,
That's what I am.

Suzanne Atkins (12)
King Edward VI Five Ways School

A Well Thought Out Gimmick - The Zodiac

Magazines have them, newspapers print them daily,
Paying someone who says they can predict the future,
Filling people with worthless ideas, saying this and that will happen,
Do you believe them and go out and act them out?

Well I read mine the other day and it said money was coming my way,
And did it happen? I fear not.
The stars and planets could not have been in the right line,
Or maybe it was not the right time, or perhaps it was never going
                                                                to happen anyway?

Look into my crystal ball, I see mist and nothing more,
I fear your future may be grim, it's in the playing cards you see.
It sounds pretty stupid when you say it bluntly,
But this is the sort of thing people take to heart and act upon all
                                                                   the time.

Your destiny is in your own hands,
You can't read it and then more to the point, believe it.
You create your future and whether you are Scorpio, Pices or Leo,
It does not matter, and Mercury being in line with Saturn won't
                                                                 change anything.

The Fire, Earth, Water and Wind symbols are pretty though,
And you can certainly get some cute merchandise with them on.
Saying things like, 'buy me and your dreams will be answered.'
In fact, there is a whole shop dedicated to them in town.

However, many people don't agree with them,
You can guarantee people will continue to read them,
Thinking maybe, just maybe, they might come true,
But you can bet all you want, they never do.

Jodi Dixon (13)
King Edward VI Five Ways School

ZODIAC

There was a circle of animals
Which decided your fate.
Which one you are
Depends on your birth date.
Aries, the ram,
May push the pram,
Taurus, the bull,
Life's problems does he pull.
Gemini, the twins,
Their football team gets many wins,
Cancer, with a pincer here and there,
Seems to concentrate on their hair.
Leo, the lion,
Is good at lying,
Virgo, the virgin,
Commits the least sins.
Libra, the balance
Is good at dance.
Scorpio, with a sting in the tail,
When someone meets him they go pale.
Sagittarius, the archer,
Goes on a departure.
Capricorn, the goat,
Has a fear of a boat.
Aquarius, the water bearer,
Hairstyle's quite a scarer.
Pisces, the fishes,
Have a lot of wishes.
The zodiac circle means love, hate and war,
To be used by everyone, well-off or poor.

Reece Somers (12)
King Edward VI Five Ways School

WEIRDO

I feel sorry for the weirdo who writes the zodiac
Who has to think up rubbish and wear an anorak,
Who thought that people would appreciate
Unreal stories of general hate.
Who cares if they are Aries,
And visited by fairies?
I feel sorry for the weirdo
With boring stories of death and heroes.
Who would really want to know
What happens to them when they go?
And anyway, if they did,
They'd be disappointed like a kid
And any normal person can see
That they'll go to work and eat their tea.
Who needs some spotty weirdo
To tell them where and when they'll go?
There really is no destiny
Except to work all your life like a bee.
So if you read the zodiac,
Go and buy an anorak.

Daniel Knowles (13)
King Edward VI Five Ways School

ZOIDIAKOS KUKLOS

Planets and stars,
Pluto and Mars,
They're in the sky,
So very high.

Twelve sections in all,
Like a huge hall.
Each has a name
That I cannot explain.

That strip in the sky
Makes me sigh.
The zodiac is there,
Neither plain nor bare.

Ayaaz Nawab (12)
King Edward VI Five Ways School

THE HEARTBREAKER

Dancing through the constellations,
Virgo weaves her rope of stars,
Brimming with romantic visions,
She leaves a trail of broken hearts.

Thoughtfully he stumbled blindly,
Aries, he was always faithful,
First but far from last, she tamed him,
The queen of hearts, forever graceful.

Taurus, strong and sensible,
Feet set firmly on the ground,
His earthy nature kept him sane,
While heads were rolling around.

Chaos reigned when Capricorn
Stepped into the skies above,
The wise were right when they said
Only fools will fall in love.

But then into the Milky Way
Came witty Libra, for the snatch,
His balanced nature and perfect karma
Broke Virgo's heart - she'd met her match.

Sally Cooper (14)
King Edward VI Five Ways School

WHAT ARE WE LIKE?

Gemini can be cool and be smart, can love to have time apart from their friends and the midday rush, they like the sound of a soothing hush. No noise to their ears is really great, they always avoid things they hate. A Gemini is good for some quiet, unless your kind of thing is a riot.

Like a Cancer who's fun and silly, get ready guys, you will be dizzy, from their dazzling vibes you will be shocked and with them you'll
be rocked.
Like a ship on the open sea, they're rough and wild and like a child. They're great for a good night out, unless you really stress and doubt.

Like a Leo who moans so much, even from a single touch on a place they don't like, they will just say 'take a hike'. They seem to know what's going around from a whisper or a tiny sound. I think it's fair to say they have gossip every day, they can tell you lots of secret stuff, but don't listen, if it's about you, you'll get the huff.

Like a Virgo who enjoys to groan, putting on an angry tone, loves to make you stressed as long as they will look the best. But they can be good for winning a debate, that will make them a good mate. They always put in lots of time to a piece of work that isn't fine, they will always be two places ahead and sorry you might be in bed.

Like a Libra who loves their room, to leave bed early would be doom. Sport just isn't their thing and they don't call, you have to ring, to tell them this and that, even though they will be sat upon the couch, sitting and probably leaning with a slouch, don't rely on them for stuff it's most likely they will rush, the morning before it's handed in. Trust me you will not win. But they can be good, if you don't like it, you should.

Like a Scorpio who is quite bad, they might laugh behind your back. In lessons they talk and sing until they can hear the lunch bell ring. At sleepovers you just can't sleep, you stay awake, they always chatter, Their jaws must ache, whenever you are bored, they will talk and try to make you smile, unless you have run off a mile.

Like a Sagittarius who loves sport, they know all there is to be taught, They can hit balls with just one shot, it will disappear in the distance Like a tiny dot. And the cleaning isn't a chore, they find it an activity they would do lots more, to be their friend they will teach you the basics, even if you're bored to bits.

Like a Capricorn who keeps themselves hidden, loud people they despise. They tell them that? No they wouldn't, this would be too mean, The people would mind, those Capricorns are kind, they wouldn't dare hurt another, to make someone cry, why would they bother? They have no one that they can't stand, people are all great whether they're white-skinned or tanned, but they might be too shy, maybe like this you might die.

Like an Aquarius who's loud and mad, I think it's hard for them to be sad, they're fun and really crazed, their whole life is a daze. From when they're born, they're moving around and dancing to every sound, they will sing to every song, even if they're old or young. Being their friend will be so funny, but not for people who hate spending money.

Like a Pisces who makes their gifts, walks down the stairs and hates the lifts. Valentine's Day is to them so cool, they go so soppy you can see the drool hanging from their mouths, when the person walks past who they fancy at school. They find animals so cute and spiders and snakes make them puke. To be their friend, they never get mad, however you can work, good or bad, but they're not for people who get stressed when they don't do their best.

Like an Aries who loves to do well, to get lower than an A would be hell. They find that if they think, problems soon start to link, they then will find them less hard and to do it will be easier than writing a card. Their good brain helps them a lot, they always come out on top. They can help you all day, unless you want things your way.

Like a Taurus who loves the spotlight, they must always be right. They can dance, sing and act, their limelight talents must be up to scratch, the centre stage, all eyes on them, will make them happy again and again. To be their friend you must be outgoing and up for showing to lots of crowds. That I doubt.

Renna Mubarak (12)
King Edward VI Five Ways School

ZODIAC MAN

Who thinks up the zodiac? Who thinks up the rules
To tempt and trick those stupid fools?
Who thinks that a tall, dark, handsome stranger
Will come and rescue them from danger,
Or that they will win the lottery tomorrow,
Or that this is the week for sorrow?

Do they have visions of what will occur
To each and every him or her?
Does every astrologer think the same,
Or is there only one to blame
For all the things that will happen to us,
From walking the dog to coming home on the bus?

So next time you go to take a peek,
Just think of the one who sits every week
And is strapped to the desk and made to write
About the twelve star signs and everyone's plight!

Harriet Smith (13)
King Edward VI Five Ways School

A SKY OF SIGNS

Look up into the velvet sky at night,
For there shines a majestic light.

The stars merge together to reveal a shape,
Is it the scorpion, the ram or the bull they create?

The signs of the zodiac are the signs of our birth,
That shine in splendour over the Earth.

The animals that are in the sky,
Also upon the Earth do lie.

Leo, Pisces and Cancer are the chosen few,
That give a bright and shining starlet view.

The signs of the zodiac are the signs of our birth,
That shine in splendour over the Earth.

The scales, the maiden and the goat,
Are Capricorn, Libra and Virgo.

Lastly are Gemini and Sagittarius,
That share the night sky with Aquarius.

The signs of the zodiac are the signs of our birth,
That shine in splendour over the Earth.

Maryam Sharif-Draper (12)
King Edward VI Five Ways School

EVERY DAY

Your life revolves around the moon,
The stars will guide you,
Every day.
Be a mystic, be a believer,
Join the club.
You must read your horoscope
Every day.
You can win the lottery,
Every day.
You can win a new car,
Every day.
And when you get to the top of the world
And see that the stars are so close
And the moon is so bright,
We will be there.
We are the people of the zodiac,
We write the horoscopes,
We want you to believe.
So,
For your in-depth daily forecast call
0906 4 710 710 (£3.49 per min.)

Thank you for your money.

Laurie Young (13)
King Edward VI Five Ways School

THE ZODIAC

I don't believe in it, do you?
Have any of them ever come true?
This is what they write:
Today is your lucky day, or
Is this a day of dismay?
You need to find your inner self,
Go to the doctor, check your health,
If you don't feel well
Take a day off,
But your boss will probably be a bit rough
With you and what you did
Just because you felt a bit dim,
Are these horoscopes really true?
Do they tell you,
Or do you depend on them every day?
Or do you go to your friend and say
That everything's gone wrong
Or is it just a myth made by the sound of a bong?
In China where they depend on them
To repair lives, we condemn
Them in the west
To make the rest
Of their journey on their own,
To find their one true home.

Yury Villalonga-Stanton (13)
King Edward VI Five Ways School

THE ZODIAC WILL GET ME

I do believe my star sign,
The zodiac, that too,
For if I say it's rubbish,
They'll come and get me, yes it's true.

The zodiac will get me,
Torture me in bed,
Flush me down the toilet,
Make sure I don't get fed.

You see it happened, while in bed,
I said the zodiac was false,
Suddenly the lights went out
And I could hear my pulse.

A bleating voice said, 'We're not fake.'
It was Aries, the ram,
'And if you don't believe the zodiac,
We'll turn you into ham.'

Leo, the lion, stood by my bed
And roared his message round the room,
'If you do not believe us,
Then evil will surely loom.'

Sagittarius shot an arrow,
Knocked a painting off the wall,
Then added in a cruel voice,
'Don't believe us and you'll fall.'

The others added messages,
Lastly Gemini,
Who added as a reminder,
'We are the zodiac, we do not lie.'

I do believe my star sign,
The zodiac, that too,
For if I say it's rubbish,
They'll come and get me, yes it's true.

Rachel Fennell (12)
King Edward VI Five Ways School

HOROSCOPES

Those horoscopes are rubbish,
I think they're a waste of time,
Nobody needs them,
Without them we're just fine.
People changing all their plans
'Cause of those stupid lies,
Can you really imagine all those things,
Up there in the skies?
Those people just don't realise
How stupid they really are,
Trusting their whole, entire fate
To a tiny, sparkling star.
My sister reads those horoscopes,
She buys them every week,
And if she finds that something is wrong,
She'll give her life a tweak.
Those horoscopes are rubbish,
I think they're a waste of time,
Nobody needs them,
Without them we're just fine.

Laurence Sutton (14)
King Edward VI Five Ways School

SIGNS

Capricorns are quiet and in the background,
Not wanting to join in, not wanting to be found.
They reach their goals eventually,
To them power and wealth make one reality.

Aquarians are idealistic and free,
These things make them quite difficult people to be.
They always think of others first,
They don't know when to stop, they've got a kind of thirst.

Pisceans are poetic and artistic,
They try to get out of difficult situations, quick.
Pisceans are loving and romantic,
Whatever you want they'll consider it.

Arians are fiery and can be violent,
They are looked upon as a tyrant.
Arians always try to get to the top,
If their anger builds up enough, they might pop.

There are many other signs,
But for those I don't have time.
Now this really is the end,
If I kept going, it would drive me round the bend.

Ben Cryan (12)
King Edward VI Five Ways School

ANIMALS

Around the Arctic ice pack occur
Polar bears with their fluffy fur.
Colours ranging from yellow to white,
Sending seals in a hysterical fright.

Tiger cubs with their stripy suits,
Sometimes so small and cute.
They have eyes of amber and gold,
Extremely skilful and bold.

Giraffes are big, giraffes are strong,
Giraffe's necks are very long.
Giraffes get an excellent view,
If you were that tall you would too.

Dolphins swimming in the sea,
Bottle-nosed, two or three.
Diving around with skill and grace,
Nearly as smart as the human race.

Camels with one hump or two,
Might be tempted to spit on you.
Treat them nicely, treat them right,
Or else you might get a nasty bite.

Daniel Carter (12)
King Edward VI Five Ways School

STORMY NIGHT

A forked bolt of electric light
Illuminates the sky at night.
A rumbling clap follows soon,
Advancing clouds obscure the moon.

First a spot, then a splatter,
Heavens above begin to shatter.
Dirt tracks turn into mud,
Roads and rivers start to flood.

Dripping drainpipes, gurgling gutters,
Anxious tenants bolt your shutters.
Swelling streams, bursting brooks,
Close your eyes, read your books.

Fearful for your heart and soul,
Mind the crashing telegraph pole!
The gale is raging through the town,
Gates and fences mostly down.

Then as quickly as it came,
The beast so wild became so tame.
The danger's gone, the danger's past,
Go up to bed and rest at last.

Our solar friend from up above,
Will spread through us with warmth and love.
The day will bring the vibrant dawn,
A new tomorrow will be born.

Mark Graham (12)
King Edward VI Five Ways School

NONSENSE ANIMALS

The fastly, fistly, foostly frog
Jumped and jibed and jubbered one day.
The gibbidy, gobbidy, gabbidy goose
Dancingly, prancingly wanted to play!
The happily, hoppily, hoopily horse
Noisily, boisily, doisily sat.
The swimmingly, swammingly, swummingly shark
Jamingly, whamingly put on his hat!
The pomingly, pimingly, poomingly penguin
Dabily, dobily, dubily donged.
The kabily, kobily, koobily cat
Maddily, middily, muddily ponged!

The oppily, appily animals were;
Fastily, fistily, foostily,
Jumpingly, jibingly, jubbingly,
Dancingly, prancingly,
Happily, hoppily, hoopily,
Noisily, boisily, doisily,
Swimmingly, swammingly, swummingly,
Jamingly, whamingly,
Pomingly, pimingly, poomingly,
Dabily, dobily, dubily,
Kabily, kobily, koobily,
Maddily, middily, muddily, there!

Penelope Thomas (12)
King Edward VI Five Ways School

IN THE SUPERMARKET

Families rush in
Through the automatic doors,
Starting their shopping.

Millions of items
All stacked neatly on tall shelves,
Then kids mess them up.

Many large sections
In the huge supermarket,
All neatly labelled.

Moms chase screaming sons,
They run smiling, joyfully,
They want yummy buns.

Completely jam-packed,
People spending much money,
They need things to eat.

Bored shop assistants
Make people pay lots of cash,
Few enjoy their job.

Broken store trolleys
Ram into tall piles of beans,
They fall everywhere.

The loudspeaker blasts,
'Would all people please leave now.'
People start to leave.

People leave the store,
Children cry, 'Please, let's not leave!'
They go through the door.

Giuseppe D'Amone (12)
King Edward VI Five Ways School

THE MATCHES

Pig takes the ball,
Giraffe takes the bat,
Monkey is fielder,
So are Cow, Horse and Rat.

Pig takes a run up
Cat behind the wicket,
Cat counts to three
And they start to play cricket!

Over on the other field,
There is a stunning sight.
One team's dressed in red and green,
The other in blue and white!

Cheers start the game,
The ball gets thrown in,
Sealion is the goalie,
The striker is Dolphin.

Midfielder is Octopus
And defence is Owl,
The first goal is shot
And the audience howl.

Ten minutes later,
Rhino takes a pen,
He kicks the football,
But it's saved by Hen.

The game ends at last,
From the final goal,
The cup gets lifted
By Duck, Fox and Mole!

Eva Quigley (12)
King Edward VI Five Ways School

Zoo

The playground's a zoo,
Kids acting like animals,
I walk round and see:

Two boys are fighting,
Lions scrapping over food,
Using all their might.

People jumping around,
A gang of mad gorillas;
Crash! Bang! What a noise!

I stroll past three girls,
Giggling like wild hyenas,
Chatting like monkeys.

Kids playing football,
Gigantic, charging rhinos,
Pushing and shoving.

Children climbing trees,
Apes searching for bananas,
Squirrels seeking nuts.

The shrieking bells ring.
Like elephants, the children
Trudge back into school.

Animals have gone,
The silence is deafening,
There is no one left.

Peter Massey (12)
King Edward VI Five Ways School

TWIN TOWER NIGHTMARE

It was a cloudless day in New York City,
A day when anything was possible,
When disaster struck and tore lives apart.
It soared out of the alluring sky
And soon exploded and hell unleashed.
The innocent, confused and afraid,
They were fastened behind a locked door.
Their life a flight of stairs away
On a runway to end very shortly.
You could miss an action when you blink,
The terror was not going to halt there,
It was going to finish its duty,
Shortly the worst was going to emerge,
This nightmare was not complete.

Suddenly an eruption occurred
And the towers sank towards the ground
Ending with a result of clutter,
Concluding with love burning in flames,
Resulting with the worst possible,
This tragedy was surely manmade.
Sparkling with joy there is a crafty grin,
A villain cheering to casualty
Who slips away in the darkness.
We mourn in the shadow of their light,
This is a disgusting nightmare,
A dream which is unforgettable,
A delusion we cannot awake from,
But this nightmare is still not complete.

Sabina Pawar (12)
King Edward VI Handsworth School

WHITE ASYLUM

In the blank, white walls the scream of captivity and
                                    disillusionment echoes,
Supposed safety hides in the acid-lemon smell of disinfectant,
Where only hostility is rife.

A blank, white nurse escorts a deep red man,
Red of the blood that scathing marks and Cassandra's gift have
                                    left upon his vermilion soul,
Bound with blank, white chains.

The garnet man is called by colours, calling to be free,
But without their crimson host to guide them,
They are forcibly clad in white.

The death-white walls are singing,
Singing their song of force and insanity,
The death-white walls are shouting,
Shouting, 'The colours of life are not welcome here!'
White is the ruler, the sovereign, the king.
White is the tyrant.

Katharine Perry (12)
King Edward VI Handsworth School

GOLDEN SUN

Hey, look at that shimmering sun,
The yellow, golden, bright orange sun.
Its ray of light pours gently down on me,
I'm as warm as can be.

Hey, today will be a sizzling day
And I'll make sure of that.
No clouds, no rain, no thunder or lightning,
Just pure delight of sun.

Hey, today's going to be my day,
I'll make sure you'll all be drenched,
My bitter rain will take over today,
No matter what any old forecast says.

Ayushah Khan (11)
King Edward VI Handsworth School

LIFE

What is life?
Is it a mystery, a game or reality?
Is it true about what people say, that we are being pulled on strings
By someone up there, high above?
Is life so precious that we can value nothing else but ourselves?
People say to enjoy your life, but do you know
That it is yours and not someone else's?
Who is the one that fiddles around with my life and yours?
Who is the one who gives us happiness, but sadness too?
Is it God?
If it is, then do we suffer from our own bad deeds,
And does God only lead us through life,
But the path which we choose is up to us?
Life is like a game in many ways, you take one step at a time
But you never know what or where the next step is.
Life is something which may involve many years and
Yet can be taken in a matter of seconds.
Living in fear, happiness, sadness, warmth and luxury,
Insisting on looking forward to the future,
Fighting against any hurdles one might encounter,
Enjoying life, no matter what,
And last, but not at all least, *living life!*

Jaspreet Bilkhu (13)
King Edward VI Handsworth School

AFTER THE CRUSH

Truth,
The realisation of truth.
An awful, alarming concept.
Drowning in my emotions,
Tears rolling perpetually down my cheek,
I am angry, confused and embarrassed,
I feel manipulated:
Not by him, but by love.
I hate love!
I feel abused,
I feel weak and vulnerable,
Irrational, humiliated, hostile to the outside world,
I am a pitiful, pathetic girl with
Dreams
So implausible, so incredible that they could not hope to be real.
Shamefully, I face the outside world, afraid of how it
Will respond to me.
My mother consoles me, my best friend cries with me,
Life assures me of another dawn.

Jenny Meszaros (15)
King Edward VI Handsworth School

THE INEVITABLE

Let it commence.
The sky becomes a deep spectrum of colours,
We know not of what we do and have obliterated,
However,
IT still remains in existence; secure in our guts.
No creature admits IT but knows of its hidden pathway.
The door remains open.

Some glance back and seek for IT; while others . . .
The sequence of the inevitable has begun.
A smile curls upon . . .
Relief is warmly injected into my soul.
I attempt in my grasp for safe reality, where am I?
Confused?

Aniqa Alam (15)
King Edward VI Handsworth School

VOYAGE INTO SPACE

Head for the stars,
Venture into space.
Round Venus and towards Mars.
And then from Europa, Jupiter's moon,
Jump down to the swirling surface
Of the mighty giant.
Sail away on an icy comet
And be guided by the cosmic angels.
Fly with them past the lonely planet Pluto,
And into the space unknown.
Take a round trip of the universe,
Past nebulas, planets and stars,
Before heading back to the Milky Way.
Climb the caters of Earth's moon
Before spiralling down,
Twisting, turning,
Down to the surface of Earth,
Home.

Kwan Yee Wong (14)
King Edward VI Handsworth School

MY PRISON

My prison is a room,
This place is not behind bars.
My prison is a place where I am stranded,
I can never escape.
This place changes every day.
My emotions change from sorrow to exultation.
This place keeps me from independence,
I am trapped here forever.
This place is inside me and around me.
My prison is a room of thoughts.
These thoughts can be mirthful and morose.
My thoughts change in this prison,
This prison is where I never go.
However, I am still there every hour of every day.
My prison is my soul, my friend, my fear, my enemy
And myself.

Nisha Ranga (13)
King Edward VI Handsworth School

TWIN TOWERS

T   otal destruction,
W orld comes to a standstill,
I   n everyone's hearts is panic,
N othing else is talked about.

T   error struck the world,
O ur problems seem insignificant.
W ednesday, still recovering people,
E   veryone is trying to help.
R eassurance from other countries for help.
S hould there be another war?

Oeiisha Williams (15)
King Edward VI Handsworth School

DUKE

My dog's name is Duke and he's funny,
His nose is ever so runny.
He sneezed up the wall
And on my brother's football.
If we let him, he would sit on the bunny!

My dad took him out for a walk,
To the butcher's they went, for some pork.
Dad told him to 'Stay,'
And the dog said 'OK.'
Well! I didn't know dogs could talk!

You may think my pooch is quite mad,
But his tale is really quite sad.
Abandoned was he,
All alone to be,
So we bought him in March and he's glad.

When he can, he jumps in the car,
Even when we are not going far.
It's got to be said,
He thinks it's his bed,
And he sits in the back like a star!

Sometimes there can be a bad smell,
From where it comes, who can tell?
My mom blames my dad,
And it makes him quite mad,
Because the dog blames my dad as well.

So now is the end of my tale,
Before my poem goes stale.
Forgive me, Miss Barker,
My dog ate your 'Parker'
But please don't send him to jail!

Rebecca Robotham (13)
King Edward VI Handsworth School

SEPTEMBER 11TH

I may not be a Muslim
But I will not be told
That a whole religion can be blamed
For a single person's fault.
Bin Laden is suspected
Of being behind it all,
But now people are blaming
Muslims, one and all.
Bin Laden has supporters,
George Bush has his own,
These groups are not divided
By your skin being white or brown,
Not by religion,
Or colour of skin.
A decision
Should come from within.
I may not be a Muslim,
But I will not be told
That a whole religion can be blamed
For a single person's fault.

Jenni Bickley (12)
King Edward VI Handsworth School

THE NIGHT FULL OF FEAR

The air was cold, the night was dark,
The striking lightning could eat a shark.
I knew that I could not get away
From this thunderous storm heading my way.

The wind full of rain and icicles of night,
I then heard a howl which gave me a fright.
The grass full of snow, glistening white,
I then was sure the storm was tonight.

My room was dark, as dark as can be,
I looked out of my window, it was an owl I could see.
The trees were swaying, side to side,
I then woke up, everything was fine.

Kavina Nijjar (11)
King Edward VI Handsworth School

LOOKING FOR GOD

I'm looking for God.
Is he big, is he small,
Is he everything we do,
Or nothing at all?

I'm looking for God.
Can I see him, is he there,
Is he a man in the sky,
Or a spirit everywhere?

I'm looking for God.
Can he feel me, can he see me,
Does he guard over trouble
And does he really love me?

I'm looking for God.
Is he there through good and bad,
If God controls everything,
Then why am I sometimes sad?

Now I've found God.
I can't see him, but I feel him.
I trust in him and now I know
He'll be there through thick and thin.

Jenny Owen (12)
King Edward VI Handsworth School

GRAVEYARD

Cold was the night,
And dark the sky,
The owls were hooting
As they were flying by.

All was silent,
All was sound,
Until I heard something
Under the ground.

What is it?
I was in doubt,
We'll have to wait
And we'll soon find out.

It sounded like bones rattling,
Coming from down under,
Are the people really dead
I wonder?

No one ever knew,
If all the people were dead,
Imagine if they weren't,
But still lying in their deathbed.

Even if they were alive,
In that earth, soft, brown and cold,
Wouldn't be much chance of surviving
Probably by now covered in mould.

Bodies half eaten,
What's left covered in decay,
All twisted and knotted
Soon all will be eaten away.

The graveyard always quiet,
As if it hadn't got a friend,
Always bored and lonely,
As if it were abandoned.

Nisha Ajimal (11)
King Edward VI Handsworth School

GROUND ZERO

A normal, golden, working day begins like any other,
To be prematurely ended, destined never to recover.
When terror and death flew in from an unclouded sky
To shake the world's complacency, cause humanity to die.
From our safe and cosy distance, we cannot turn away,
Cannot believe the horror, cannot think of words to say.
Images of a modern Armageddon are flashed around the world,
A giant cloud of choking dust is suddenly unfurled,
Rising like a malevolent beast to swallow up a tower;
The symbol of enormous wealth, a citadel of power.
The scenes resemble an action film, repeatedly being played,
But there is no indestructible hero here so that everyone can be saved.
Day turns into night, all colour is drained away,
As if time itself has stopped, everything fades to grey.
Through the dust of dark oblivion, a few survivors stumbling come,
Like spectres with blank, unseeing eyes: shocked, disbelieving, numb.
But hope for other survivors gradually withers away and dies,
No matter how determinedly the tireless rescue worker tries.
Now the world considers to see what action it should take
To defeat the terrorists' reign for the future of all our sakes.
These daunting nightmare images, these deaths demand a price.
Is it revenge or justice that we seek, the ultimate sacrifice?

Charlotte Florance (13)
King Edward VI Handsworth School

THE WORLD

At first there was peace in America,
Everything was so calm,
But as the busy people did their duties,
Lots of lives came to harm.

The silent, blue sky
Was suddenly awakened by deep thunder
As evil entered the atmosphere,
The good fell down under!

Thousands of people were injured,
No happiness was left in their life.
Families are left devastated,
Like they had been stabbed by a knife.

How can people be so cruel
As to do such a crime?
To pierce someone's heart.
Why should they have a lifetime?

Emma Prendergast (11)
King Edward VI Handsworth School

CHOCOLATE

Chocolate is the best thing in the world,
It's good as a present to a friend,
You can eat it on its own,
Or give it to someone who is driving you round the bend.

Chocolate comes in many flavours,
Dark chocolate, white chocolate, milk,
Big ones, small ones, square ones and round ones,
Some in a box tied with a ribbon of silk.

Chocolate is my favourite food,
I like milk chocolate, but white is nice,
I'm not too keen on advent calendars,
I especially like little, white mice.

I would never give up on chocolate,
It is the one thing that keeps me alive,
Whether I was tortured or dragged in hot sand,
Or thrown into a bee's hive.

Hannah Vawda (12)
King Edward VI Handsworth School

LOOKING FOR GOD

Is God really here in our world,
Or is he in heaven with a white beard of curls?
Does he look down on us day and night
With his loving son, Jesus, at his right?

Should I look for him in the trees or in space,
Or is there some other special place?
No, go and look in your heart,
Until you are no longer apart.

Why is God a spirit for us not to see?
Look in your heart and you'll find the key.
God protects you from all your fear,
Every hour, day, month and year.

God loves us all just the same,
One day in heaven we'll meet him again.
All you need to do is trust and seek,
You can't see God because he's unique.

Alison Hearn (12)
King Edward VI Handsworth School

THE TRUTH ABOUT ST GEORGE AND THE DRAGON

Once upon a time they say,
A fat and lazy dragon lay.
He had an awful reputation,
His name sent fear through every nation.
His body, it was huge and scaly
And he breathed out great flames daily.

Now at this particular point in time,
The dragon had captured Caroline.
This princess was kind and caring,
And was excellent about not staring.
She was also very refined and pretty,
And everyone said she was rather witty.

Due to this awful situation,
Knights were sent in from every nation,
Including one whose name was George.
(You have heard of him, of course.)
George was neither kind nor clever,
His name goes down in history forever.

George rode off to slay the beast
Who was enjoying a tasty feast.
The knight strode up and drew his sword,
The creature sat on his hind legs and roared.
George stabbed his sword into the dragon,
Who fell and landed on a wagon.

The princess hurried out of the cave.
It was clear that she was very dismayed.
'What have you done, you blithering fool?
That dragon was really very cool?
He was always kind and sweet,
You do not deserve to kiss his feet.'

Jenny Tasker (13)
King Edward VI Handsworth School

A Better World

Does anyone even care
When there is crying of despair?
Families torn, hearts begin to ache,
Puddles of tears turn to lakes
From the evil in this world.

Simple grudges turn to hate,
Try to turn back, but it's too late.
When hate has you, it makes you strike,
Makes you do things you really don't like.
That is the evil in this world.

Bombs, guns, knives, all weapons to use,
Your caring self gone, there's nothing to lose.
You strike, stand back,
Your world has turned black.
You're part of the evil in this world.

Asking yourself why, oh why
Did I really bother to try?
I've let my grudge get the better of me,
I was stuck, blind, I could not see.
There should be no evil in this world.

Hate can get out of hand
And harm everyone in the land.
Terrorists and others open the door
To a sick beginning, a brand new war.
Why is there evil in this world?

Lifting corners of your mouth to make a pretty smile
Can change sad impressions, at least for a while.
End all grudges, we don't want a world forlorn,
Start a new friendship, happiness is born.
Now you can see no evil in our world.

Sinitta Flora (13)
King Edward VI Handsworth School

HE SAID HE COULDN'T STAY LONG

So he opened the door.

I didn't want him
to see the spider web cracks
in the grimacing plaster,
or the shameful ivy snapping away their faces
in disgrace.

He walked in regardless,
brogues ripping back
threadbare carpet from the uneven planks,
man hands groping
for the baby limb stair rail.

The walls blushed scarlet
as his heavy feet left an imprint
of each great digit on each warped step
as if it was sand
but permanent.

The rickety frame sobbed
through gritted teeth and bitten lips
and he carried on walking,
feeling his way as it got darker
up the narrow passageway.

He didn't turn back
so I sat on the doormat until he had finished.

Lucy Machon (17)
King Edward VI Handsworth School

THE STARS

Every night I look outside of my bedroom window,
There I see sparkling shimmers of light,
Creeping through my flower netting,
I see dots of these lights spread out equally.
The dots, they shimmer and fly through the sky,
I thought they were little fairies,
Now I know they are beautiful sparkles called stars.

Annika Ranga (11)
King Edward VI Handsworth School

AUTUMN

Like a colour chart without paper,
Bug-green, rusty-red, chocolate brown,
Like a sunset that has just met the horizon,
Tipped with orange and embroidered with pink,
A patchwork quilt for Mother Nature
When the last light has gone out
And the world turns from light to darkness,
When the last bird has stopped twittering in a tree
And the white paw stops rustling through
The undergrowth beneath.

The tree's bark studded with a brown-crested fringe,
The leaves veined with cotton,
Twisted and turned painfully,
The seams of the patchwork.

Rachel Webb (12)
Kings Norton Girls' School

THE EARTHQUAKE

I heard a cry and then a shout,
Out of the pipes the water came out,
The dust-covered mud soaked it up,
No clear water to fill our cup.
Under the house lay Mum and Dad,
The fireman going under it, were they mad?
In a split second they'd be dead too,
I wouldn't go under, would you?
They are dead already, why go under?
They're not even in a deep, deep slumber.
My leg is stinging like mad,
I can't bear to look it's so bad.
I've lost count of the people dead,
They were all just lying there while they bled.
My brother's lying dead in his destroyed room,
I was watching TV when I heard a big boom.
I am all alone in this destroyed place,
The loss of my family I cannot face.
There will be no Christmas this December,
This event will be something I will always remember.

Kirsty Davies (12)
Kings Norton Girls' School

IS THERE MORE TO YOU?

In the back of an old magazine,
They tell us what to do.
The only time it happens,
Is when you want it to.

Aries, Scorpio, Gemini and so on,
Does it really matter much?
It's just the day you're born on.

Cancer, Capricorn, Aquarius too,
Does your personality fit,
Or is there more to you?

This matters to some people,
But not to me,
I live my life as it's meant to be.

Eleanor Browning (12)
Kings Norton Girls' School

ALL ALONE

There I was, all alone,
Wishing I was back at home.
Creeping about, I wonder why,
Will anyone pass me by?

Someone grabs me by the shoulder,
Turning round slowly and getting colder,
As usual, it's just my imagination,
What a horrible creation!

Still creeping but getting braver,
I open a door and find a paper.
I feel a chill on the back of my neck,
I know someone's following me,
Waiting to give me a deck.

Then suddenly I wake up,
Sweating more than ever,
I reach for my cup
Knowing I need to mend,
But is this the end?

Charlotte Creba (13)
Kings Norton Girls' School

TOMCAT

Sleeping on his owners' bed,
Not moving at all, he looks like he's dead,
Still hiding his fierce lion-like eyes,
All around you hear his cries.

When half the world is fast asleep,
He walks out of the house not making a peep.
Suddenly he makes a very sharp jump
And catches a mouse, which he'll take to the dump.

In through the park showing his catch,
Hopefully now he'll meet his match,
When out of nowhere comes a terrible growl,
A puppy-like panther that's on the prowl.

Bearing his sharp, spiky fangs,
Other cats bunching up in gangs,
His claws as sharp as rattlesnakes' teeth,
Cutting into his enemy beneath.

Lying dead is the enemy cat,
Bloodstained areas where it had sat.
Tomcat is the champion one,
Now he's glad the dead cat is gone.

Home he goes 'cause it's nearly morning,
The humans will soon be up and yawning,
In through his flap he goes once more
And lies in his basket next to the door.

Penny Bourne (13)
Kings Norton Girls' School

MY STAR...

My star sign is Capricorn,
It brings me luck for all.
It promises me a millionaire
Just like a questionnaire.
There's always a time when romance kicks through,
The love and tenderness it promises you.
My one and only brings me luxury
When the storm clouds tell me
I'm there one and only.
I'm so practical in every way,
I'm like the sea floating away.
What I live on I don't know at all
But my lucky colour is yellow,
I should be called a marshmallow.
My lucky number hasn't pulled through,
I will tell you my number, number two.
I have told you my luxury hasn't pulled through,
But soon it will, I promise you.
I'm all I am, just like you,
I'm Mrs Stephanie Smyth from Mary Vale Road.
Not just then, not just now,
It will come true somehow.
I wonder, I wonder on yonder star,
This represents playing with a car.
I begin to get colder
When I grow older.
Please say how I pray on my own with a rose.

Stephanie Smyth (11)
Kings Norton Girls' School

Paranoid In The Dark

As night comes
A shadow casts across the sky,
The only light is in the dark outside.
The stars shine as a blanket,
The moon shines down like a giant light,
But you shiver in your room in fright.

The house is silent,
Nothing is heard but the trees
Swaying in the darkness, you feel weak at the knees.
Your door creeps open,
You can't breathe any more,
Then a shadow appears on the door.

You see a glimpse
Run past your eyes
As you hear a cry slowly die.
You look around, there's nothing there,
The sound is horrific, as you want to scream,
Trying to make out it is all a dream.

The floor seems to sink
And you feel quite dizzy,
Things running round your head, feeling all giddy.
You sit down to take a breath,
Looking round, gasping for air,
Waiting for morning to forget this nightmare!

Yasmin Fearon (13)
Kings Norton Girls' School

The Glorious Match

Football, football is the best,
I like it more than all the rest.
The referees are very sad,
Their decisions make me mad.

The crowd like to sing and shout,
To watch the players pass the ball about.
The managers are always cunning,
They make the players do all the running.

Kelly Johnson (12)
Kings Norton Girls' School

STAR SIGNS

Aquarius,
Strong, witty and faithful.
Pisces,
Sensitive and loving.
Aries,
Confident and quick.
Taurus,
Patient and protective.
Gemini,
Young and weird.
Cancer,
Protective and loving.
Leo,
Encouraging and calm.
Virgo,
Shy and quiet.
Libra,
Charming and kind.
Scorpio,
Forceful and calm.
Sagittarius,
Intelligent and wise.
Capricorn,
Peaceful and giving.

Michelle Harris (12)
Kings Norton Girls' School

WHY?

Why is the moon round?
Why is the sun so bright?
Why is it that mice give elephants such a fright?
Why are some people more talented than others?
Why are we here, what do we fear?
Why do we do the things we do?
Why do we kill?
Why do we cheat?
Why do we kill animals but not for meat?
Why is there day?
Why is there night?
Why isn't night light and
Why isn't day dark?
Why are we old?
Why are we young?
Why do we fade away?
Why for everything do we have to pay?
Why do we ask these questions,
That's something we'll never know,
We'll hurry across the surface of the Earth,
Rushing to and fro.

Elizabeth Cooke (12)
Kings Norton Girls' School

LEO THE LION

The lion wakes up from his long sleep.
He yawns as he uncurls out of his heap.
Getting ready for his hot, fierce summer,
He knows that the deer are getting dumber,
Just the right time to go tracking.

Knowing that the lions are behind, backing,
He runs up on the herd,
But the squawks give him away, from the birds.
But the next time they aren't as lucky,
He goes home all mucky.

Katy Proctor (12)
Kings Norton Girls' School

POP GROUPS

S Club 7 go wild,
As well as Destiny's Child.
Five are now out,
Blue are about,
Hear'say are the thing,
Linkin Park blast their singing.
Steps are in a chain reaction,
Limp Bizkit are in action.
Westlife are cool,
They make everybody drool.
Atomic Kitten are the best,
Somewhat better than the rest.
Kylie's number one was brill,
Michael Jackson's back to give us a thrill.
Allstars definitely make me smile,
Hope Robbie will be around for a while.
Britney Spears is at her best,
She's putting Christina to the test.
All these stars are worth their weight in gold,
Millions of copies of songs they've sold.

Katy Marshall (11)
Kings Norton Girls' School

ON MY OWN

I sit here on my own,
Wondering what will happen.
The rain will start
When all is dark
And nobody else is awake,
Just me, on my own.

In my bedroom I'll lie awake,
Until up to bed they come.
Quick, I'll think and close my eyes
And dream of the days
In my perfect ways,
Where I will be alone.

Laura Carroll (13)
Kings Norton Girls' School

MY MATES

When life gets you down,
Just turn to your mates,
They won't let you down.
If you've been stood up on a date,
Your mates will wipe away the frown.

They're good for gossip, sleepovers too,
But most of all they're friends with you.
So whenever you feel unhappy,
Just give your mates a ring
And you'll soon be feeling happy,
You'll feel you want to sing.

Laura Batsford (12)
Kings Norton Girls' School

LIBRA

Librans are thoughtful, kind and caring,
They take time to think,
To make things link.
If you stick them on a scale,
They would both weigh the same.
They are all clever and
None of them are lame.

Librans, Librans, how can I explain?
They are sometimes good and sometimes a pain.

Librans are active, happy, not sad,
It makes you just want to go mad.
In the future I foretell
That one Libran will build a hotel.
The business is a hit, not a miss,
But we still have lots of bliss.

Librans, Librans, how can I explain?
You're sometimes good and sometimes a pain.

Louise Colin (13)
Kings Norton Girls' School

UP IN SPACE!

Stars, they twinkle up so high,
Up in the sky, I want to fly.
The sun, it's bright and boiling hot,
But Pluto is cold, hot it's not.
There's lots and lots of planets in space,
And such a lot of open space.

Hannah Freemantle (13)
Kings Norton Girls' School

ZODIAC

Zodiac star signs what are you?
Do you think you're a Libra?
Think again, for all you know
You're a Pisces until you read this poem.
Aries, a sign of fire ruled by planet Mars, headstrong and implosive.
Taurus, a sign of Earth ruled by Venus, loving and good-natured,
Gemini, a sign of air ruled by Mercury, talkative and
                                        changeable moods,
Cancer, a sign of sun ruled by the moon, sensitive and home-loving,
Leo, a sign of fire ruled by the sun, generous and protective,
Virgo, a sign of Earth ruled by Mercury, talkative and shy,
Libra, a sign of air ruled by Venus, thoughtful and intelligent,
Scorpio, a sign of water ruled by Pluto, secretive and energetic,
Sagittarius, a sign of fire ruled by Jupiter, optimistic and generous,
Capricorn, a sign of earth ruled by Saturn, shy and fun,
Aquarius, a sign of air ruled by Saturn, open-minded and friendly,
Pisces, a sign of water ruled by Jupiter, dreamy and creative.
I'm a Capricorn, now do you know what you are?

Nicola Ashmore (11)
Kings Norton Girls' School

THE SUN

Your flaming hot coat
Covers you as you float,
Your shine so bright
That if I look at you,
You destroy my sight.

You're ever so high
In the deep blue sky,
With all those planets turning
And your heat burning.

You warm the whole world,
So we're not cold,
Thanks to your rays,
You light up my days.

Danijela Kastratovic (12)
Kings Norton Girls' School

RIVER FLOW

From start to finish,
Day to day,
The river flows
Through country villages.
Like the seasons,
Coming and going,
The river flows.

From start to finish,
Day to day,
The river gushes.
Joining valleys and streams
Along the way,
Getting bigger and wider,
The river gushes.

From start to finish,
Day to day,
The river flows.
Past fields filled with heather,
Fields full of sheep,
The river flows,
Down to the sea.

Kellie-Marie Windsor (13)
Kings Norton Girls' School

SIGNS OF THE ZODIAC

Are you the lion of Leo,
A fearsome, feline, fine?
Are you the crab of Cancer,
Small, sharp and silent,
Or are you the scorpion of Scorpio,
With a sting in your tail?

Are you the virgin of Virgo,
A pretty, patient girl?
Are you the twins of Gemini,
With a split personality,
Or are you the fish of Pisces,
A fast, frantic fish?

Are you the bull of Taurus,
With a nasty streak in you?
Are you the goat of Capricorn,
A lively life in you,
Or are you the ram of Aries,
Always raring to go?

The zodiac will know.

Fay Newman (12)
Kings Norton Girls' School

STARS

S   tars all around the world,
T   winkling so brightly and so proud,
A   lways wondering how they stay up,
R   uling the whole universe, helping us to find our way,
S   himmering in the sky and smiling throughout the days and nights.

Charlotte Burch (13)
Kings Norton Girls' School

STAR SIGNS

Look out for double the trouble,
You will all want to stick them in a bubble
Or at least something that can't pop.
You will never want that bubble to stop.

They will always want to play lots of tricks,
They will always get crosses, not ticks,
They are naughty, not nice,
They will always go for the dearest price.

Geminis come in twos,
You will never find any clues
Where they have been,
They will be nowhere to be seen.

You won't ever know where they are heading,
But they have probably gone clubbing in Reading.

Lauren Allen (12)
Kings Norton Girls' School

LIFE!

Why do we stop?
Why do we stare?
Why do we do things
That pull us down into despair?
Why do we do things by a rota,
Why not by chance?
Why do we take things for granted?
Why do we call this life?

Elizabeth Rose (12)
Kings Norton Girls' School

MY KATZ

I have ten katz,
They're nothing but trouble,
Nothing bur fur.
They have two round, blue eyes,
They have a giant purr,
But only a tiny mew!

They love chasing each other,
They like a ball,
But they don't care
For a mouse at all.
None of them really!

There's Ginger, Pickles
And Millie and Fluffy,
And Whiskers, Mittens,
Toady and Fluffy.
Oh yeah, Molly and Holly.
I guess I love all ten!

Laura Greenway (11)
Kings Norton Girls' School

BIRTHDAY

Birthdays, stars, symbols and signs,
Fish, bull, crab and ram too,
All lived together, tightly as one,
Hold on tight 'cause the galaxy's just begun.

Taurus, Aries, Sagittarius, Leo and Cancer,
January, March, April, June, July and September,
Both linked together are called star signs,
Everybody's comes at different times.

One, three, five, seven, eight and thirty-one,
Fire, air, water and earth too,
It's quite weird, don't worry, I know
Some day you'll have your go!

Everybody has their own special day,
Whether it's tomorrow, next year or today.
Every year it'll come around,
Regular as clockwork, straight and sound.

Ashleigh Devine (12)
Kings Norton Girls' School

WHERE?

Sunset's setting across the sea,
Sound echoing closely,
Moon's shining brightly through,
Cliffs hanging, like it too.

Wishful thinking your trust in mine,
Climbing mountains, snow nearby,
Dream and screaming,
What will happen now?

Shops closing, ready for night,
On go the glittering lights,
So shut my eyes and go to sleep,
But not until I've cleaned my teeth.

Stars sparkling across the sky,
Discovering my thoughts and why
I shed a tear but nothing comes out,
To why I had this day.

Jade Atterbury (13)
Kings Norton Girls' School

The Fortune Teller's Warning

A red and white striped canvas of mystery, delusion,
An open curtain beckoning me into secrets, confusion.

The fortune teller's tent.

A lady ordained in bracelets and beads,
Willing to tackle your problems, your needs.

The fortune teller.

A glass ball, delicate and reflective,
Showing the type of life you may live.

The crystal ball.

The signs, the symbols spinning round and round,
Taurus, Pisces, faster than a merry-go-round.

The zodiac.

Capricorn, the goat, is ambitious and will work hard,
Leo, the entertainer, shouts out, 'Pick a card!'
The list continues, Virgo, Pisces the fish,
Cancer the crab, answering your every wish.
Aries, Libra, Taurus, curious Sagittarius, good with money,
Insists on saving it in tins.
Then the sixth star sign, Gemini, the identical twins.

But beware.

Beware of Aquarius, the water bearer, no love will he send,
Unpredictable, single-minded be warned, you may meet him at your end.

When flames rise from the depths of hell,
When discomfort and fear you begin to smell,
Beware of Aquarius.

The fortune teller cried.

Laura Preece (11)
Kings Norton Girls' School

THE THIRTEENTH ZODIAC SIGN

There are twelve zodiac signs,
All who have a special name and rhyme,
But somewhere around,
A thirteenth sign cannot be found.
His name is Thirteen
And for six hundred years he has not been seen.
Thirteen is unlucky and it started like that,
How this sign slipped as low as a rat.
He looks like a shadow, but he's really a man,
A bit of white hair and a brilliant tan.
So now you know, the secret is out,
If you see someone when you're out and about,
Don't stay there, move along or run,
Before he shoots you with his magic gun.
Shooting stars will shower the crowd,
Great - until they swear out loud.
So you see, this sign is nothing but bad,
The zodiac sign who makes the other signs mad!

Rachel Galloway (11)
Kings Norton Girls' School

THE ASTROLOGER

'Now, what shall I write today?'
The famous astrologer said.
'Today, I will write about Aquarius,'
He pulled out a book
That had been hidden in cranny and nook.
He read aloud,
'Aquarians good, honest, true and loyal,
And very spoilt.'
He reached for his notepad and pen
And started scribbling down notes.
'That wasn't very true,'
He sat in his chair and thought hard,
'It's unfair
For all those people to believe
What I'm writing,
When it's all just predicted.
There are too many people out there
For just one paragraph of information
To relate to everyone.'

Beth Hiscock (12)
Kings Norton Girls' School

I DON'T THINK SO!

Libra, Virgo, Leo too,
Which star sign are you?
Bossy Leo, thoughtful Virgo,
I don't think so.
All they do is make it up.

Mystic Meg's crystal ball
Doesn't predict anything at all.
Your destiny will guide you (as if),
All it is, is a silly myth.

Libra, Virgo, Leo too,
Which star sign are you?
They make it up, that's all they do,
Or you never know, it could be true.

Rebecca Glover (11)
Kings Norton Girls' School

DREAM ON

In my dream
I'm all alone,
Not knowing if I'm at home.
Somewhere distant I could be
Looking out as far as I can see,
No one there,
Except for me.

In my dream
I'm all alone,
Wishing that I was known.
It's just like playing hide-and-seek,
But no one seems to be finding me,
No one there,
Except for me.

In my dream
I'm all alone,
Sitting in the corner wanting to go home.
Looking upon the horizon,
My dream goes on and on,
No one there,
Except for me.

Caroline Busby (13)
Kings Norton Girls' School

OPPOSITES OF LIFE

I love, but hate,
I'm an enemy, but a mate,
I am a child, but I'm a mother,
I'm a sister, but a brother,
I am evil, but kind,
I can see, but I'm blind,
I'm smart, but dumb,
I have four fingers and a thumb.
I am here, but there
And I don't really care.
You know me, but you don't,
You love me, but you won't.
I'm free, but I'm not,
There's a gun and I've been shot.
I'm alive, but dead,
I'm asleep in a bed.
I am tall, but small,
I'm loving, but cruel,
I am ugly, but pretty,
I'm smooth, but gritty,
I am half, but whole,
I'm on top in a hole.
I am happy, but sad,
I'm sane, but mad,
I am calm, but stressed,
I'm naked, but dressed.
I am not the fashion, but I'm the trend,
This is the beginning, but the end.

Sara Hughes (14)
Kings Norton Girls' School

I'M DEAD

No one can hear me,
No one can see me,
All I can remember
Is me lying in a hospital bed.
There was a beeping, the nurse came and said,
'Your daughter is now dead.'
How did this happen?
Why did this happen?
What's happened to me?
My eyes cannot see.
I want another chance
To see my mum with one last glance,
I just want another chance
To live my life again.
To love my sister I hated so much,
To cuddle my mum with her soft touch,
All these things I want so much,
But I'll never get the chance.
God, I pray to you right now,
Can't you renew my life somehow?
Why did I deserve to go
And leave my friends and family behind?
I love my mum,
I love my dad
And the best sister I ever had.
I'm going to miss them,
Really I will,
But now I'm off to heaven
Where time stays still.
Goodbye.

Julia Wood (13)
Kings Norton Girls' School

The Zodiac

My mom used to read the zodiac all night and all day long,
So I decided I'd take a shot at it,
But it didn't help me at all.
The zodiac said I was faithful,
But no one can rely on me.
The zodiac said I was loving,
But who wants to go near me?
The zodiac said I had a strong character,
But even my mom disagrees.
I used to believe in this gibberish,
Until one day it said:
'Your destiny is riding a white horse on the moors.
It will travel through gates and pathways
To seek your innermost dream!'
I have travelled far and searched wide,
But it was nowhere in sight,
So now I know
That my destiny is a lie!

Natalie Heraper (11)
Kings Norton Girls' School

Chocolate

Creamy and silky
You can't resist,
It melts in your mouth
Like a chocolate digestive.

Lots of it is sickly,
Too much could mean fate,
But once in a while it can be vile,
But today it must be great.

Chocolate balls with foamy bubbles,
Rippling inside the stars shooting through the sky,
Straight through the middle, here it comes,
A funky, creamy taste with lots of charm.

Emma Yates (13)
Kings Norton Girls' School

FAKE

What shall I write today? Um.
Capricorn: buy that clock you have been meaning to.
(Yeah, right. People are so gullible.)
Aquarius: follow your heart to your true love.
(I don't know where I get this stuff from.)
Pisces: buy that top you saw last week.
(You won't regret it.)
Aries: a recent argument will upset you.
(Might give this up for the truth.)
Taurus: do your best in a test.
(You never know, this might be the truth.)
Gemini: read that book you have been meaning to read.
(I wish I could really tell fortunes.)
Cancer: don't fall out with your friends.
(That's got to be the best.)
Virgo: your mom's annoying you, ignore it.
(Nah, that's better.)
Libra: you have been feeling moody, get over it.
(My star sign is next.)
Scorpio: your destiny will guide you.
(As if.)
Sagittarius: don't go to that party you have been thinking about.
(I like it.)
I love this job!

Acacia Dixon (11)
Kings Norton Girls' School

LOVE

Love does such wonderful things,
You feel like an angel with wings

Love is good, love is bad,
It sometimes makes me feel glad.

Sometimes it makes me want to cry,
Or curl up, wishing to die.

Whatever happens, it should be from the heart,
To make things slow and never part.

I love you always, night and day,
I love you in every kind of way.

My love for you is always true,
I hope you feel the same way too.

Hayley Adams (13)
Kings Norton Girls' School

GEMINI

It *said* today would be a good one -
Can it be right?
I'm supposed to be getting my number one friend -
Instead I fell out with two!
I'm meant to be going in the right direction towards my dreams -
Instead, I found that the bus had been re-routed!
I read that tomorrow's my lucky day -
But I'm booked to see the dentist.
It said that an unexpected phone call will leave me smiling -
But what's so funny about *double glazing?*

Alice Jones (11)
Kings Norton Girls' School

THE STAR SIGN WRITER

Capricorn, a goat, practical and patient,
Ha!
I'll make them have a miserable weekend!

Aquarius is water, honest and loyal,
Better make it good.
The stars still hate you!

Pisces, a fish, sensitive and kind.
What? What nonsense!
The stars have something mean in store for you!

Aries, a friend of mine, still a bit strange though,
Make this one nice,
Err . . . you're being haunted by a cat!

Gemini, the twins. Which one's which?
Make this one the last for tonight,
Em . . . I'm stuck. Aww, forget this!

Avril Flower (11)
Kings Norton Girls' School

ARIES

A ries, the sign of the ram, beginning of the zodiacal year.
R anging from March to April will Aries fall.
I ntelligent, courageous and kind,
E nthusiastic and quick-witted, are you like that or are you wicked?
S ide of darkness they all possess, can be self-centred, impulsive,
                                  quick-tempered and fresh.

Emma Gossage (11)
Kings Norton Girls' School

BURNING DESIRE

My burning desire is long-lasting for you,
Like a red rose, clear, bright and new,
As the last petal falls softly on the floor,
This might mean that you don't love me anymore.

Like a flower in white snow,
Does this mean you will never let go?
Dreams are passing on and on,
Before I know it, you have gone.

I dream about you every second of the day,
I think about you in every kind of way.
When I think about you my life feels complete
And when I see you my heart skips a beat.

My love for you will always be true,
Everything I do, I do for you.

Charlotte Tisdale (13)
Kings Norton Girls' School

FRIENDS

Friends are like gifts,
They're hard to get,
They come down from God.
To lose one makes me cry.
So if we break up,
Let's make up,
I like to be friends with you,
So be my friend
And I'll love you.

Aimee Ibbetson (12)
Kings Norton Girls' School

Two Great Horses

The horses were galloping nearby,
The sun was rising high in the sky,
The river was twinkling like a thousand stars,
The horses galloped, they galloped right by.

The night had started to kick in,
The horses ran like a gust of wind,
Like ghosts of happiness breezing through,
They galloped as if there was no time.

Two were like the Queen's that ruled,
Honey was the giant of all,
As Nutmeg was a cute as could be,
They are the joy of my life
And will always be there at my side.

Hayley Reeves (13)
Kings Norton Girls' School

In The Classroom!

A rainy day,
What a gloom,
I'm stuck sitting in a classroom.
Teacher's droning on and on,
Look at the clock going tick-tock,
It's still only 3 o'clock.
People bored, I've just yawned,
No one in the world has ever been more bored.
Boys making aeroplanes,
Girls whispering one, two, three,
Ha ha, hee hee, that's so funny.
Oh no, the teacher's looking at me!

Vicky Burlison (11)
Kings Norton Girls' School

WHY ME?

Mom moans,
Dad groans,
They never let me out,
Sitting here on my own, nothing else to do!

I ask again and again,
They just keep saying, 'No!'
Why is it always me
That's never allowed to go?

Don't they trust me? What've I done?
I'm told I haven't done a thing
And when I sit and wonder why,
I sit and watch my friends go by.

I wish they would give me a chance,
I am fourteen, I'm growing up!
How long do I have to wait,
Till I'm allowed out late?

Katie Freezer (13)
Kings Norton Girls' School

MY NEW STAR SIGN

It must be large,
It must be strong,
It must be at least fifty feet long.

It must be long, grand
And play in a band.
It must look sharp
And play a mean harp.

It must be called Classic,
No, maybe Jurassic,
I know, I'll call it Inassic.

It must be kind
And always say, 'I don't mind.'
It must be fierce,
But not when it's getting its ears pierced!

Lauren Currier (11)
Kings Norton Girls' School

WHAT A LIBRA IS LIKE

I am looking through a magazine,
I am getting very keen,
Here's the column on Libra,
A little bit there, a little bit here.
As I look at what it says,
It says I am charming and
Also sophisticated in many, many ways.
The Libran's good looks and
All the merits in the teachers' books,
Make them irresistible, to be the teacher's pet,
That's why they get full marks in
Every piece of work which is set.
The Libran gets on well with Gemini and Aquarius,
But if they got on with Pisces, that would be hilarious.
Oh well, at least I know what I am all about,
I am a pretty and sensible girl
And I do not scream and shout.

Kirsty Bond (12)
Kings Norton Girls' School

MOBILE MANIAC

A Mobile Maniac is what I am,
Playing games all day long.
Every day I change the tune,
I'm getting a new case for it soon.

I play on my phone
When I am bored,
And top it up
When I can afford.

I take it with me everywhere,
To school, to the park
Even to the fair.

Laura Allsop (12)
Kings Norton Girls' School

PISCES

They're sensitive and kind,
But with a free mind.
But watch out and wait,
Because she may be keeping something from you,
Which decides if you're really mates.

Also, a hint on love too,
A special boy just for you,
But a mate's coming your way,
So watch what you say.

Enjoy the 5th to the 8th,
Because these days will be absolutely great!

Victoria Bunting (11)
Kings Norton Girls' School

BONFIRE NIGHTS

The glowing light,
Shining bright
In the night sky.

I can see explosions
Of glitter and flashing lights.

I can hear the people,
Laughing and chanting,
While they see the display.

I can feel the heat
Of the bonfire,
The colours are
Glowing in my eyes.

The display is over,
It will soon be the end,
Until next year
When we celebrate.

Sophie Keenan (12)
Kings Norton Girls' School

IS IT IN THE STARS?

Z odiac is when stars foretell,
O f your destiny, ill or well.
D o you believe it?
I s it true?
A strology, mystery, is it for you?
C onstellations near or far, can they tell you what you are?

Jessica Pritchard (11)
Kings Norton Girls' School

A New Zodiac Creature

There is a new zodiac creature
Who's smarter than any old teacher.
Although they're extremely naughty,
They are also very sporty.
They're adventurous for life,
They're husband and wife.
They will work in a factory sponsoring Adidas or Nike,
Now wait till I tell you what their star sign looks like.
It's bright and shining everywhere,
All over towns, cities, carnivals and fairs.
It's not an animal like a horse, croc or bear,
Because it's a more wonderful thing,
It's the North Star way up there.
Its day is Friday, the thirteenth is its date,
If that's your birthday, you're the new zodiac mate.

Yvonne Forrest (11)
Kings Norton Girls' School

Gandy

Twelve years ago you held me as a baby,
Your first grandchild.
You watched me take my first stumbling steps,
You heard my first attempts at words,
'Gandy!'

You carried me around on your shoulders,
I could see the whole world from up there.
You liked the stars, the sky at night,
The Plough, Orion's Belt.

On woodland walks you pointed out
The birds that fly so high.
Rare red kites at Harewood House,
The one-eyed horse at Temple Newsam,
Goats that chased you everywhere.

As I grow up, you grow old,
You can't lift me up on your shoulders now,
Longer walks are merely strolls,
But you're still my 'Gandy.'

Rebecca Jones (12)
Kings Norton Girls' School

SCARED

As I lie in my bed,
I pray and hope my dad's not dead.
When I walk down the street,
I see the fear in people's eyes,
They're just like me deep inside,
Scared and nervous
About what's to come next.
My stomach churns
When the guns go off,
I run and try to hide in shops.
I hear screaming and crying
And lots of shots.
You pray and hope your family's all right,
The feeling you get you cannot bear,
But the attackers don't care.

Helen Shaw (13)
Kings Norton Girls' School

MY FRIENDS

I love to dance and sing and shout
And love to prance about.
I love to go out with my friends
And mainly just hang out.
I love to get all dolled up right
And go out and have a ball,
And I wish everyone loved me,
Because I love them all.
A lot of my friends are very special,
Because they live far away.
I wish they were here right now
So we could go out and play.
Those would all be very special
Happy kinds of days!

Lydia Johnson (12)
Kings Norton Girls' School

CAPRICORN

Flicking through a magazine,
See your stars, go on and read.
Wonder what it says?
Who am I going to be?
Do the surprises really work for me?
I look down to Capricorn
And decide to read more,
This truth and lies it says about me.
Is this my future?
Is it meant to be?
I decided to wait for a day or two,
See if my hopes really do come true.

Alexandra Waldron (11)
Kings Norton Girls' School

DEADLY NOISES

Haunted sounds of the haunted house go on all night,
The tooting of the ghosts is a gruesome sight.
The banging of the broken shutters,
The rats' and bats' deadly tutters,
The creaking of the floorboards and rusty-hinged doors,
Zombies chopping up bodies with roaring saws.
The screams of the children who will soon be dead,
Who will rest in their silent coffin bed?
The sound of the thunder hitting the rotten window sills,
It's scary knowing there have been so many kills.
The whistling of the wind through the trees,
Gives me a shiver up the spine and shakes my knees.
Listen to the footsteps up and down the stairs,
Where you stand knowing nobody cares.

Laura Jones (11)
Kings Norton Girls' School

XYLER

Xyler, the symbol of love and trust,
Latin for the phrase 'beauty and lust.'

Xyler, Xylerians are very kind, caring and intelligent,
Always out there looking for the perfect gent.

Xyler, its perfect match is always a Taurean,
Has loads of friends who are Scorpions.

Xyler, fortune tellers say it's from the planet Pluto,
I'm not too sure if I believe that though.

Xyler, date August 23rd to the 22nd September,
I just don't know, there's something to remember.

Selina Abercrombie (12)
Kings Norton Girls' School

THE GREATEST STAR SIGN

Aries
20th March - 19th April

Your time will come to meet someone new,
A new romance is in your life, tu-whit tu-whoo,
Good luck has failed you this time,
You're tired and feel like slime.

Venus is moving closer to Mars,
Your future is held in the stars,
You have too much to worry about this week,
But don't worry, a new love you'll seek.

This is not even true.
Oh, it's only last week's.
I wouldn't believe it in any case,
To me, horoscopes are *through!*

Michele Prosser (11)
Kings Norton Girls' School

THE ARIAN

In charges the ram!
Fortune favours the bold!
Swift and intrepid,
Rams never grow old!
Houdini, Leonardo, Van Gogh, Elton John -
And me, P Andrea who's singing this song.

At best we are quick-witted,
Exciting, courageous and free.
Vincent Van Gogh and Raphael
Have the same values as me!

But when we are bad,
We are very, very bad.
Impatient, thoughtless and rude,
Sharp as a thistle, tactless and vain,
Bad Arians, what a pain!

Penny Andrea (11)
Kings Norton Girls' School

CONSULTING THE STARS

Browsing through your magazine,
Spot your star sign, if you're keen.
What will your horoscope have in store?
Will you dare to read some more?

Will it tell of fun and treats
And maybe a special person to meet?
Will it say, 'Take care today,'
In case there's something bad on the way?

Maybe it says you'll win some cash,
So you can go shopping and splash
It all on clothes and lovely new stuff,
Then collapse, exhausted, when you've bought enough!

Not feeling too good? It's all in the stars,
From Jupiter to Earth, Saturn to Mars.
Your horoscope tells you how you'll feel,
Even if you don't believe it's real.

From health to wealth, and love to life,
You read your future - even trouble and strife.
It's almost addictive, like books and TV,
You can't help thinking it's meant to be.

Anisa Haghdadi (11)
Kings Norton Girls' School

Zodiac

Signs and stars,
Venus and Mars,
Leo and Aquarius too.
Destiny, fortune and Mystic Meg,
These are all things that are pulling your leg.
Libra the balanced,
Taurus the bull,
Gemini the twin,
Which category do I fit in?
Aquarius is water, Pisces too
Will they all tell me what to do?
Scorpio, Capricorn, Aries, the lot,
Will they tell me who I am
And who I am not?
Sagittarius, what is the fuss,
When some people read their signs on the bus?
Now I have mentioned all the Zodiac signs,
They all correspond to different dates and times.
I don't think I will depend on them an awful lot,
I've read them and read them and I'm losing the plot.
I don't think I will read them anymore,
I am just finding them a terrible bore.
I've finished my poem with the zodiac theme,
Upon my face is a very large beam.
This very long poem took me a while,
But now I can rest and smile, smile, smile!

Kimberley Ohren (11)
Kings Norton Girls' School

HALLOWE'EN

The night has come, it's only just begun,
It's time to scream, 'cause it's Hallowe'en.

High up there,
High up there,
Witches, witches,
Everywhere.
Watch out,
Watch out,
There's a demon about.

Ghosts and ghouls and vampires too,
Over your shoulder watching you.
Screaming, shouting all around,
Lots of goodies to be found.

High up there
High up there,
Witches, witches,
Everywhere.
Watch out,
Watch out,
There's a demon about.

Trick or treat, smell my feet,
Please don't give me worms to eat.
Let's all go home and settle our heads,
I wouldn't even bother looking under your beds.

Manijeh Arabpour (11)
Kings Norton Girls' School

TAURUS

I flick through a magazine,
And have a read of my stars,
It says I'm patient,
But that's going far.
You see I'm really noisy and always on the go,
So that is a definite no, no, no.
My star sign is Taurus,
All gentle and kind,
That's just not me,
But I don't mind.
I can't believe people really read this stuff,
I've really, really had enough.
How can fortune tellers tell such a lie?
They're really, really, really sly.
Fortune tellers wave over a ball,
Predicting when things will fall.

Kerry Holohan (11)
Kings Norton Girls' School

RAINBOWS

Red is cheerful and fun,
Yellow is as bright as the sun,
Pink is a baby's lip being kissed,
Green is grass which has been missed,
Orange is a sunset on the sea,
Purple is a best friend close to me,
Blue is the sky on a summer's day,
Multicoloured is the wind, it blows me away.

Abigail Tomlins (12)
Kings Norton Girls' School

STAR SIGNS

I read my star sign in a magazine,
According to my star sign, I am supposed to be keen,
To be honest and loyal
And see life through original eyes.
An Aquarian never lies.

The picture to go with it,
Is a person carrying water
In a pale brown pot.

Star signs are supposed to come from the stars,
Much further than Mars!
Star signs go beyond Earth,
Star signs depend on your birth.

Kimberly Wellings (11)
Kings Norton Girls' School

TAKING HOME FOR GRANTED

Sitting at home, TVs, PlayStations, stereos,
Microwaves, freezers, armchairs and our beds,
All these in our homes
And all these, we take for granted.

But what about those hidden homes in the world
Which haven't seen a TV,
Just full of empty dreams of rain and crops,
Full of disease in the air choosing its next victim?

But in our homes all snug and warm,
We do not care about these hidden homes,
Because we take home for granted!

Lorna Brown (11)
Kings Norton Girls' School

WORD WAR II, A CHILD'S TALE

Boom, crash, boom, bang!
All through the night the thunder sang.
The sirens were wailing and whining,
And inside our houses the puppies were pining.
I hoped it would soon stop,
But still bombs would drop.
One blanket for warmth, one candle for light,
Down in that pit we sat up all night.
We opened the door in to the day,
A ghost town, some would soon come to say.
Our streets, our houses had all gone
And all because of one little bomb.
A tag round my neck and I'm on a train,
My gas mask beside me and it's pouring with rain.
An old woman and man and a farm too,
All of it seems so very new.
I know that I'll never see my mother again,
Why is it that I'm filled up with pain?
I miss my home and all of its streets
And the shop on the corner that gave me free sweets.
My father's a soldier, he'll be home soon,
He'll put a stop to this and I'll be over the moon.
Then soon, boom, crash, boom, bang!
All through the night, the thunder still rang.

Amy Farrington McCabe (13)
Kings Norton Girls' School

BIRDS

Birds in a tree
Are tweeting away,
Flying above us
And perched on the bay.

It's ready for flight,
As black as jet,
And as white as a bright light,
If only I could have met.

Katie Rouse (12)
Kings Norton Girls' School

THE POWER OF A SMILE

A sob brings a dark, black cloud sweeping and swooping over me,
Every happy thing or thought is a mere memory,
Fading fast, going, going, gone.
A cold chill settles over me,
Starting off at my heart and working, squirming through my body.
A sob stretches out and its cold touch sucks the soul out of me,
Only one thing can defeat a sob, like good defeating evil . . . a smile.

A scream reaches out and strangles me at the throat,
Shatters the world around me.
It sends torrents of rain beating down angrily at me,
Ripping and lashing at everything before my eyes.
A scream shakes my feelings around inside me,
All those things I never revealed to anybody, never wanted to
                                                          talk about,
They all bubble up and give me the urge to scream them out.
Only one thing can defeat a scream, like good defeating evil . . .
                                                           a smile.

A smile starts off like a gentle, tickling flame in my heart,
And I feel a warm glow within me.
It grows and grows until I am completely toasted inside,
I feel stronger, all my fears and worries drowned in happiness . . .
A smile makes me feel I belong.

Katarina Jankovic (12)
Kings Norton Girls' School

BIG BROTHERS

Big brothers are just such a pain,
They need a whacking with a cane.

But you can't do that anymore,
'Cause sadly it's against the law.

They hog the telly and the shower,
They stay in there almost an hour.

They stay up late and sleep too long,
I just think it's really wrong.

They fight and squabble with each other,
But sometimes they're such lovely brothers.

Rebekah Hand (12)
Kings Norton Girls' School

MIXED FEELINGS

Where the yellow tulip petals lie,
There the baby lay in cloth.
Where the two-year-old dog lay at the curb,
I strolled past without a word.

As I passed, the dog glanced in sorrow,
I picked it up, it cuddled up quietly.
I took it home, it lay in front of the fire
And fell asleep into a midnight wonder.

Whilst lying there, he was having a dream,
I saw it float out of his head
And go into a dreamcatcher,
Not to annoy his endless sleep.

Kelly Penman (11)
Kings Norton Girls' School

AT THE ZOO

A screech, a squawk, a roar,
A wing, a head, a paw,
I'm at the zoo,
There's lots to do,
I must go and see more.

I've found the tigers who are proud and strong,
Their bodies are sleek,
Their tails are long.

I'm with the emus, what strange things,
Their feathery bodies,
Their grey and brown wings.

Look at the monkeys,
Acting the fool,
Swinging around, I hope they don't fall!

Listen to the birds, their calls are unique,
Their colours are bright,
And look at that beak!

Watching the elephants having a nap,
Their bodies grey,
Their ears flap.

Be careful now, we're near the bears,
Their large fat paws,
Their bristly brown hairs.

I've seen all the animals right up close,
But I just can't decide
Which one I like most!

Sophie Hickman (12)
Kings Norton Girls' School

MY FRIEND AND I

My friend and I do everything together,
Us two.
We go to the loo together,
We play and say our thoughts together.

We get told off together
And have a bath together,
We sing songs together,
We even dance and prance together.

We like to run together,
And have a lot of fun together.
Sunny days we like to play
Funny games together.

But most of all I hope
We stay friends forever.

Charlotte O'Sullivan (11)
Kings Norton Girls' School

MY MUM

It's special mums like you
That don't just grow on trees,
That makes you feel that unbelievable feeling,
That everything is at ease.

It's the warmth of love so powerful
That goes from heart to heart,
It's a laser that dies when I miss you
Or whenever we're apart.

It just goes to show just how
Strong relationships can be,
But that feeling inside me will never change
The feeling of love to you from me.

As I said, these mums are vary rare
And very special too,
But no mum is more special than my mum,
Because no mum is more special than you.

Amy Johns (12)
Kings Norton Girls' School

SOMETHING TOLD THE WILD GEESE

Something told the wild geese
It was time to go,
Though the fields lay golden,
Something whispered, 'Snow.'
Leaves were green and shining,
Berries lustre-glossed,
But beneath the warm,
Something cautioned, 'Frost.'
All the sagging orchards,
Steamed with amber spice,
But each wild beast stiffened
At remembered ice.
Something told the wild geese,
It was time to fly,
Summer sun on their wings,
Winter in their cry.

Louise Parks (12)
Kings Norton Girls' School

I LOVE FOOD

Peas, raw, stuck on the floor,
Strawberries with cream hanging on the door.
Ham cooking in a pan,
It went all bad, so I just ran.
I love food, don't you?
Mom said, 'Tidy up your mess,
Or else I'll wipe it up with your best dress.'
My cake was baked,
With cream and jam, mmmmm!
How lovely, I have a plan.
I love food, don't you?
I like curry in a hurry,
Hot and spicy,
With rice as white as mice.
I love food, don't you?
I like jam-red ham,
With drink in a can.
I love food, don't you?
I like chocolate melted in my cup,
Creamy, slimy, slip down my throat.
Mmmmm, how lovely!
I love food, don't you?
I like tea, coffee,
With a choccie biccie,
I love, love food, not anymore!
I feel unwell,
My breath smells!
Excuse me, I just need to go to the loo!

Kelly Scott (111)
Kings Norton Girls' School

BE MINE

It was in the way you talked to me
And the way you cared,
The way you took a glance,
Even when brushing my hair.
When you touched me I felt special,
You make me feel alive,
But now you're gone it hurts,
There's nothing left inside.

I try and get along,
The lonely days pass by,
The tears sting my face at night,
Don't come back and I'll still cry.
We used to laugh,
Have a good time,
Remember the first time you came to mine?
Your face would light up and make mine shine.

The nerves were bad,
You had them too,
Can't remember how many times I went to the loo.
Didn't know what to do or what to say,
But I know now I couldn't be without you another day.
There's a hole in my roof,
The rain's coming through,
Come back and fill the hole, I'll be there for you.

You can be my sun and you can still shine,
Come back to me now, you can still be mine.

Sarah Ventre (12)
Kings Norton Girls' School

School

School is where I go every day,
Except Saturday and Sunday,
From 8:30 to 3:05,
Somehow we survive.
All the work we get,
All the homework that is set,
How do we survive?
If you want food, you have to wait in a line,
And when you have finished waiting,
You are not in class on time.
When the teacher asks why you are late and
You tell her you have been in the queue,
You're lucky if she believes you.
There are other things about school,
But you'll have to find out for yourself.

Sheryl Pagan (11)
Kings Norton Girls' School

When?

Yesterday would be tomorrow,
If tomorrow were today,
But today would be yesterday,
If yesterday were tomorrow.
So tomorrow would therefore be today,
If today were yesterday.
Have I lost you yet?
I've lost myself.
Words that don't make sense at all,
Or do they?
Read again, what does it say?
Is it nonsense or sensible?

Samantha Moore (13)
Kings Norton Girls' School

ME

My eyes are the stars,
My nose is the moon,
My lips are a crib for a child so young.

My arms are the trees,
My fingers are the leaves,
My palm is a bird floating in the breeze.

My legs are dolphins diving in the sea,
My feet are my roots, holding on steadily,
My heart is a cloud as fluffy as can be.

My soul is Earth,
My spirit is birth
And all of them together make me.

Chloe Amoo (12)
Kings Norton Girls' School

THE LADY

Standing with her flaming torch,
Now in broken bits on a porch.
She watched her city disappear,
Wondering if it will ever reappear?
She watched her city burn to the ground,
She never even made a sound.
She was a lovely lady,
She might come back, one day maybe.
The lady of Venice was very grand
Until she came crashing down on the land.
She was gone,
And all because of one little bomb.
May there be peace everywhere.

Rachel Doherty (12)
Kings Norton Girls' School

MY RABBIT, SNOOPY

The date was 16th October.
My rabbit died yesterday.
All through the cold night,
I thought about her,
Crying in my room alone,
Then wondering where Shady,
The other rabbit was.
Where is she?
Is she alive,
Or what's happened to her?
At the bottom of the garden,
I will dig a hole and bury her,
As a memory to me.
I still love her.
RIP.

Lauren Spencer (12)
Kings Norton Girls' School

SUNFLOWERS

Sunflowers in my garden,
Starting to grow, to begin,
Rising high above all others,
Never-ending, 'til they win.

Like giants they tower above us,
Bright and full of life,
During the day they follow the sun,
To catch all of its light.

The sun is their master,
They follow from east to west,
At night the sun goes down
And the sunflowers' heads all rest.

Sunflowers in my garden,
Starting to grow, to begin,
Rising high above all others,
Never-ending, 'til they win.

Alice Ridgway (13)
Kings Norton Girls' School

TEENAGERS

Teenagers to some people may seem crazy,
And yes, I know they can seem lazy,
But put yourself in their shoes,
Their lives have just begun,
They are out partying, having loads of fun.
Upstairs in their very messy rooms,
Parents getting angry as their music booms,
Dancing wildly, making the lights shake,
Parents groan and wonder how much the floor can take.
And yes, you've told me once their clothes don't always look great,
And okay, most of the time they are always late,
But put yourself in their shoes,
I bet you wish you could.
Those years don't last forever,
I bet you wished they would.

Sophie Lawrence (13)
Kings Norton Girls' School

MY MATE MARY

'Secondary school really isn't scary,'
That's what I thought,
Till I met my mate Mary.

Mary was that kind of girl
Who was obviously rich,
She even gave me a great big pearl.

We had been at school for about two weeks,
I was getting along fine
Until I heard two great big shrieks.

I was walking home
When this thing jumped out,
Dressed as a giant gnome.

Then I saw that it was Mary,
Shoplifting from a shop
On the great Canary.

Mary was clutching something tight,
I looked closer,
But it was too bright.

That's when I noticed what she had done,
She'd been getting things
To make new friends at our new school.

Emma Stiff (13)
Kings Norton Girls' School

SPARKLY, SPANGLY

Sparkly, spangly disco diva,
Got loads of glitter on, have you seen her?
High heels, short skirts and covered in make-up,
I wish the boys would hurry up and wake up.

She can dance, she can sing,
She can do everything!
She's a fashionable girlie and likes Lee,
I like him too, what's wrong with me?

Leah Murray (12)
Kings Norton Girls' School

EMOTIONS AND AMBITIONS

When I dance, my world disappears,
I forget all my sorrow and my tears.
When I move, I forget what's there,
I see only me, I do not care.

When I act, I feel so alive,
When the audience applaud I feel a vibe.
When I perform, I put on another act,
I am no longer me and that's a fact.

When I am with my friends
I have so much fun,
Once again, my youth has begun.
I laugh, I smile, I giggle and I gossip.

When I shop, I cannot stop,
I want trousers, shoes or even a top.
I test all make-up and look like a fool,
But to me, it looks really cool.

When I go to clubs, I feel mature,
I dance all night and look great, then when it's finished
I just wait for the next one to come and it will all have begun,
I will be the dancing queen and have loads of fun

And they are my ambitions and emotions.

Charlotte Williams (12)
Kings Norton Girls' School

I'M GLAD I'M A CAT!

I'm a fluffy, fat cat
Sitting on a rug
In front of a fire,
Warm and snug.
Out in the garden,
It is dark and bleak,
My fur stands on end,
I hear a shriek
In the darkness,
A shadow quivers,
It sends down my spine cold shivers.
I fall asleep peacefully dreaming,
I pounce on a mouse,
I hear it screaming.
I suddenly wake up,
Not dreaming any more,
I see some wool
Slither across the floor.
I chase it and pounce,
My prey unaware,
I am glad I'm a cat,
I haven't a care!

Lucy Willetts (12)
Kings Norton Girls' School

SEASIDE

Sea is blue, clear and cool,
It has lots of fish, dolphins and more.
When I go to the seaside,
I wish I could be there all the time
And paddle with fish
Swimming through my toes.

But when it comes to going home,
My feet are stuck to the sand.
Oh no!
My mom and dad put me in the car,
I'm going now,
Bye-bye, t'ra!

Abby Field (11)
Kings Norton Girls' School

IT WAS BETTER IN MY OLD DAYS

Looking across the street today,
Many things have changed,
New jobs . . . more yobs!
New laws . . . more wars!
It was better in my old days!

In my old days there were no cars,
And none of this new 'web,'
It was plain and simple, easy to live,
Are you listening, Deb?

'Yes Gran, but a horse and cart
Won't get you to town,
I know modern technology makes you frown.
Computers are great, tellies are fab,
The old times are so drab!'

Looking across the street today,
Many things have changed,
New jobs . . . more yobs,
New laws . . . more wars,
It was better in my old days!

Elizabeth Sanders (12)
Kings Norton Girls' School

BONFIRE NIGHT

Coloured sparks,
Lighted flames,
Bonfire night is a danger game!
Sparklers fizzing, crackling, turning,
Rockets blazing, brightly burning,
Shooting up through the night,
Setting twigs and leaves alight.
Flames roar and fireworks whizz,
Blasting off with a bang and a fizz.
Frightened faces, terrified,
As deafening bangs blow up the sky.
Animals running, yelping, hissing,
Wishing that they could be missing
This scary, loud and weird night,
Flames that flicker and fill us with fright!

Emma Lewis (12)
Kings Norton Girls' School

HALLOWE'EN

Hallowe'en, Hallowe'en,
The scariest night you've ever seen!

When you feel a shiver down your back,
Get ready for the Hallowe'en attack.
Trick or treaters roam the streets,
All they want are tasty treats.
Scary movies, cool decorations,
All for the Hallowe'en celebrations.

Hallowe'en, Hallowe'en,
The scariest night you've ever seen!

Leila Milne (13)
Kings Norton Girls' School

SCHOOL, HERE I COME!

The greatest fear in the world is starting secondary school.
All the teachers seem so nice, but you're wrong.
Some can be very strict, in fact willing to give demerits out!
They give you loads of homework,
So you're up till 12 o'clock,
With thousands of questions and problems to be solved.
As you walk around the school,
The feeling of being the oldest disappears.
You feel like a baby once again among the older kids.
I must confess the dinners are lovely,
Massive choice of different kinds, English old!
Wordwide and meat free, of course.
The last and worst thing is the weight of all the books,
Which make your spine shrink!
After all, secondary school can't be too bad,
You've just got to get used to it!

Olga Milkiewicz (11)
Kings Norton Girls' School

THE BEST SCHOOL DISCO

At the school disco, I sat all alone,
I decided to go, so I got out my phone.
Then out of the blue came a handsome young lad,
His name was Lance, and he asked me to dance!
He bought me some pop and he gave me a sweet,
My friends were so jealous that they all could not meet.
He dropped me off home and he gave me a kiss!
We went to the pictures on Friday,
That was definitely my day!

Madeleine Sanderson (11)
Kings Norton Girls' School

MY BROTHER

My brother went away last week,
The house was really quiet,
I'd forgotten that my brother could
Cause such a riot.
Picking his nose, he sits in the corner
Reading the Beano and thinking of Shauna.
His girlfriend is ugly, he hasn't got a clue,
He stinks the whole place out while sitting on the loo.
His clothes are outrageous,
He's certain he can't lose,
But boy, if he could see himself,
I know he'd blow a fuse!

Elizabeth Hodgkinson (11)
Kings Norton Girls' School

ANGER

It froths up deep inside of you, you let it escape,
Scaring everyone and everything,
Like a tiger pouncing on its prey,
Ripping it to shreds and then chewing and swallowing.
Creeping up and attacking you when you're not looking,
It is a ghost, a shadow, a spirit, it is lots of different things.
You know when it is ready to swoop.
It makes me think of suffering, of blood and dying,
Seeming like the world is ending when it decides to strike,
Covering everything with its dark coat, making everything miserable,
It makes it seem like all is lost.

Jessica Grant (13)
Kings Norton Girls' School

THE LITTLE BIRD

Soaring through the moth-eaten bark,
Over the rocky earth,
Across the silvery, glistening streams
And dodging the long, swishing branches.

I make my way into this beautiful garden
Overflowing with all sorts of wildlife.
At last I am free from the city's traffic,
In this breathtaking world of peace.

I swoop down low with my breast feathers just skimming the ground
And land softly on the light, fluffy soil.
I spot a juicy, pink worm a few yards ahead,
I hop over, swipe at it and slurp it down in one go.

Uh-oh, I can sense danger ahead,
A cat strolling along the cobbled path.
I panic and take off to the nearest branch
And wait until it has gone.

I think it better to get out of here
And leave this glorious garden to its peace,
So I wait until it is all clear,
Then I hop over to the garden wall.

I take off onto the grey, dusty road,
But see bright lights ahead - coming closer.
I flap my poor wings as hard as I can, but I don't get anywhere,
Then . . . *thud* . . . it all goes black.

I didn't get away from all that city traffic then,
Maybe that garden wasn't my dream destination after all.

Beth Collett (13)
Kings Norton Girls' School

THE ONLY THING TO SEE

A coral rock looks out to see the only thing to see, sea.
Above it tall and mountainous is a cratered pearly rock
Tossed with evergreen weed, and tiny pebbles that scatter from
                                        the ocean blue.
Emerald patches show up the bottom of the glistening cove and
Coat it with light as the sun shimmers around.
Rain droplets hit the ocean as bullets hit a wall.
They bounce right back and spray leaks from the ocean.
Waves crash and claw the sand into the ocean ready for fresh life.
The summer's here, no winter breeze and frozen leaves, no cold water
And no more silent days, not filled with sounds of life.
Upon a cliff at the nearby cove, gulls screech and animals scuttle and
Through the light of a child's eyes, we commune and see
What it's like to live by the sea,
To open our eyes and explore the sky, while the rock on the shore just
                                          looks by,
Where the grass is green and the sand is golden,
We look and see the only thing to see, sea.

Kirsty Rostill (12)
Kings Norton Girls' School

HALLOWE'EN

The clock strikes twelve,
The graveyard starts to wake,
The ground moves,
The gravestones shake.

The beasts are coming,
Vampires, zombies and all,
They come to kill,
Some fat and some small.

They break into houses,
Vampires bite necks,
The witches make curses,
The homes are wrecked.

Then the clock strikes one,
Some people are dead,
Some are injured,
Others are still hiding under their bed.

Emily Meades (12)
Kings Norton Girls' School

THE DAILY STARS

The stars move left and right,
They heave and push with all their might
To bring you your daily stars.
Go get the paper, go in your car,
You'll find a boy or even a friend
That sometimes drives you round the bend.
You'll find something new, a hobby or two,
A scary nightmare, new to you.
Maybe love or a tragic thing,
Is it true the things they bring?
All is unreal with the stars,
This is the truth, it's all bizarre.
When's your birthday, July or June?
Whether you're young or an old prune?
We all buy mags with horoscopes in,
Sometimes we keep them or throw them in the bin,
But the thing is, we all read them!

Joanne Griggs (11)
Kings Norton Girls' School

THE WEATHER

The weather's fine, the sky is blue,
Not a cloud to spoil the view.
Now what's happening in the sky?
Cumulus clouds are coming by.
I feel a shiver down my spine,
Will the weather now stay fine?
That bright blue sky has disappeared,
Here comes the rain, just like I feared.
The sky is dark and full of rain,
Oh, it really is a pain.
The wind is really blowing now,
Will I stay dry? I don't know how.
I've left my brolly and my hat
Sitting on the hallway mat.

Hayley Rock (12)
Kings Norton Girls' School

A TRIP TO THE ZOO

I went on a trip to the zoo,
I saw a big kangaroo,
It jumped so high,
It started to fly
And landed on zookeeper Sue.

I went to the lions' den,
There was a lion there called Wen,
She roared so loud,
It made a big crowd
And she scared my friend called Jen.

Then I went to see the deer,
They were all drinking beer,
But it was time for me to leave.
Please don't any of you grieve,
Don't worry, because I live near.

Sophie Hall (11)
Kings Norton Girls' School

MY TREE

Since I can remember, that tree has been there.
Every year it grows a little, every month it has a new leaf,
Every day I look at it with interest.

In autumn, the leaves change colour to orange, red and brown,
They look as pretty as a picture,
Because all the leaves are different.

In winter, the leaves go brown and hard, then they fall silently
to the floor,
The tree looks bare, but that's all right,
As I know it will soon be beautiful once again.

In spring, the leaves come back, one by one they slowly uncurl,
The greenness becomes brighter as the day goes by,
The tree is almost the same again.

In summer, the leaves are the brightest you have ever seen,
The flowers are in blossom; the tree is like a picture.
Silently the wind blows, making the leaves rustle.

The autumn is my favourite season,
The tree is just right,
I wish I had planted that tree for everyone to see.

Laura Jackson (13)
Kings Norton Girls' School

THE NEW YEAR

Three, two, one!
An excited cheer fills the room,
Poppers explode, streamers are thrown,
No one miserable, no one in gloom.

Singing, dancing, drinking champagne,
I take a look at my family and friends,
Forgetting their troubles, enjoying themselves,
Looking forward to making amends.

I step outside, the cold air hits my face,
Snow is on the trees, which glisten in the moonlight.
In the distance I hear a few parties,
Fireworks banging purple and yellow, disturbing the night.

What will the New Year be like?
Will the troubles be left behind,
Or will they still hang around us?
They will probably stay in my mind.

My mother's voice interrupts my thoughts,
'Darling, you're missing out on the celebrations.'
So I put my worries at the back of my head
And enjoy myself with my friends and relations.

Laura Hardy (13)
Kings Norton Girls' School

MY FAMILY

'Who's this?' I said to Uncle Ned,
'Oh that is you, crying in bed.'

'Who's this?' I said to Aunty Bower.
'Oh that's your mom, picking a flower.'

'Who's this?' I said to Grandma Daisy.
'Oh that's your cousin who's really lazy.'

'Who's this?' I said to Grandad Dule.
'Oh that's your aunt who's really cool.'

'Who's this?' I said to Cousin Dotlut.
'Oh that's your sister who loves her chocolate.'

'Who's this?' I said to Nanna Loast.
'Oh that's your brother who's scared of ghosts.'

Emily Heel (11)
Kings Norton Girls' School

THE MONKEY IN MY HOUSE

I live next to the zoo,
With the lions and kangaroo.
The animals are funky,
Especially the monkey,
But he's always saying, 'Boo!'

I hear them at night
As I turn off my bedside light.
They all fall asleep,
But the monkey still peeps,
As he swings from a dangerous height.

The monkey swung over his cage
And got the lions into a rage,
Then he walked down the path
With his monkey laugh
And swaggered like he was on stage.

He walked into my house,
As quietly as a mouse
And opened the cupboard,
Like Old Mother Hubbard,
And ate till he started to grouse.

Rebecca Farman (11)
Kings Norton Girls' School

LOOKING GOOD?

Walking to the hairdressers,
Came my biggest job,
Hmmm, what to choose,
A perm or a bob?

Entering the door,
Hearing the bell ring,
I stand and look at the piccies,
Waiting for Mrs Bing.

As Mrs Bing approaches,
Dates book in her hand,
To know this is the moment to choose the 'do'
That makes me look like a million grand.

Mrs Bing adjusts the chair height,
Making sure I can see
My reflection in the mirror.
Last time I look like this,
Last time I look like me.

Hearing the snip,
My hair on the floor,
Feeling nervous,
I glance at the door.

My hair,
Trimmed and curled to perfection,
With this hairdo,
I could win any election.

Jess Edwards (11)
Kings Norton Girls' School

MY STORY

A lot of things have I experienced.
Both my moms murdered,
By one man!
I was a princess, and then I was queen,
Now . . . just an ordinary person, just like you.
The town I ruled was destroyed by him!
All I have left are my friends and my life.
I do not know my fate yet, unlike some people,
I hope it's not as bad as my past.
It's hard to remember what happened,
My mind is flooded, like an ocean deep,
With bad things and nothing but . . .
For now, I hope good times lay ahead of me,
My love shall grow for one boy.
For now, I depend on my friends
To rescue me from my nightmare.
I wonder if this nightmare will end?
For all I can think of is myself.
I want more emotions than just sadness,
I want to think of life in other ways,
Instead of death.
All I think of is 'I want'.
My friends and I are scared in case,
In case one of us dies.
For now, I shall destroy my enemy,
For my destiny is revealed.

Kathryn Taylor (12)
Kings Norton Girls' School

CHARLIE, OH CHARLIE

Charlie is a boy I met last year,
He has got blue eyes and curly hair.
One day, he made a terrible disaster,
Charlie, oh Charlie, what have you done?

This disaster was very big,
He came to school in a dress and a wig.
I pretended I wasn't with him that day,
Charlie, oh Charlie, what have you done?

We then argued because people took the mick,
I will *never* forgive him for that day.
People laugh at me just because of him.
Charlie, oh Charlie, what have you done?

You don't know how I've been feeling since that day,
I have been all alone since then.
I'll never make any friends now,
Charlie, oh Charlie, what have you done?

Rachael Priest (11)
Kings Norton Girls' School

THE PLANETS

Mars, Pluto and Jupiter are just three of the planets' names.
There are six others beside them, who all play different games.
Well games they don't play, so to speak,
They hang around in space, all week.
Saturn with its colourful rings,
Spins about in space, without any wings.
Neptune and Mercury are two other names,
Both of whom play different games.
Uranus is not as rude as you think,
In fact it is green and blue, not pink.

Two planets we have left, one Venus,
The other is the one that'll never leave us.
Of course, it is called the planet Earth,
The number one planet, because of my birth.

Anna Harris (11)
Kings Norton Girls' School

MY FAMILY

My brother is a half-wit,
He is really horrible too,
He is really thick and stupid,
I don't know what to do.

My mom is really nice,
Beautiful and caring too,
She cooks really delicious food,
I really love her, yes I do.

My dad doesn't care,
Drinking loads of beer,
Sitting on the couch all day,
He hasn't got a career.

My nan is very busy,
Knitting or watching TV,
Chatting with her mate
And laughing herself silly.

My brother, I really hate him,
I pushed him on the floor,
He is still there crying,
Now we both know *this means war!*

Louisa Hitchen (12)
Kings Norton Girls' School

WHAT COULD IT BE?

I have a little secret
You'll really want to know,
I found it in the attic under my old pillow.
It was rusty and dirty and made a loud clang,
When I opened its door, it gave a mighty bang.
I don't know how it got there,
Until I got inside.
It flew me to Jupiter and then the planet by its side.
It was dark and musty, I couldn't see a thing,
Then I turned to the side and saw the gleaming beam.
With my right hand I pressed it,
I waited for the drop,
I could feel my belly turning
And my ears went pop.
I opened my eyes and the first thing I saw
Was the wall of the attic and our old, grey door.

Lorna Nickson (11)
Kings Norton Girls' School

ZODIAC

Zodiac, zodiac, zodiac,
What does this mean, zodiac?
Owner of planets, future and luck,
Moon cycle, star sign, Leo and Scorp.

Planets, Mars, Saturn and Jupiter,
Men are from Mars 'cause they're stupider.
Future, past, present or never,
Travel in a time machine made by the clever.

Moon cycle, planet, future and luck,
Caring and loving to help when you're stuck.
Star sign Leo, Libra or virgin,
Leo am I, 'cause I am determined.

Eno Umotong (11)
Kings Norton Girls' School

THE ELEMENTS

Fire burns like the sun in the sky,
Many people often ask why?
I turn to them and simply reply,
Because it's an element of life!

Water is fun, to wash and to play,
You use and drink it every day.
In the river it flows away,
But it's still an element of life.

Earth is what lies beneath your feet,
The most amazing thing you'll meet.
It makes everything, from food to a seat,
Another element of life.

Air you can't see but you know it's there
And to hold your breath, you wouldn't dare.
It floats around without a care,
The final element of life.

All these things give us life,
Without them we would surely die,
Suffocate or turn to ice,
These elements give us our life.

Katie Jowett (12)
Kings Norton Girls' School

A FLOWER'S HALLOWE'EN

I am cold, discoloured and lonely,
Blowing in the wind on this Hallowe'en night.
Looking in on the houses, people eat their supper,
Followed by sweets and delights.

Oh, why does it have to be Hallowe'en?
The night is lit only by the moon.
The television screens flash from one screen to another,
The children will be coming out soon!

A group of children walk down the dark, silent streets,
With a lantern, all wrapped up warm,
Knocking on doors, hoping for chocolates and sweets,
The freezing homeless wearing rags that are torn.

Early fireworks explode in the distance,
Filling the sky with pretty pinks and blues.
The children run on, down to the next door,
Splattering mud on their shoes.

My stem snaps in half in the wind,
But no one cares, which makes me uptight,
I am lonely, unwanted and ugly tonight,
Parents looking at the fireworks sight.

Just past midnight, all the witches gone by,
Ghosts in the air make a scary atmosphere.
The smoke from the bonfires fills the cold and spooky air,
As people from a house make a cheer.

The smoky air floats around and warms my petals
As a gang goes past across the grass.
My body is crushed into the muddy, green field
And this unwanted breath is the last.

Kirsty Dodwell (12)
Kings Norton Girls' School

Jungle

The birds are singing as sweet as honey,
The monkeys are swinging fluently,
All the animals live in harmony.
The rustle of leaves on the green floor
Sends a startle up my spine and leaves my hairs high.
A glint of gold as bright as the sun,
Far beyond where I have come,
I squint to see what it is . . .
Tiger! Tiger! Run, run, run!
An enchantment comes over me, I can't run.
The tiger runs with death intent,
Its powerful legs are a train's wheels.
The tiger's breath comes to me,
Its claws are daggers as they pierce my heart,
I smell the stench of its breath as it devours me.
Now . . . black, nothingness.

Jack Kirk (11)
Moseley School And Language College

My Poem

There's no one like my bossy brother,
He acts just like he's my mother.
He's got a pair of dirty black socks
And his clothes go in a box.
He wears a black Timberland hat,
He is a fat, short, ugly brat.
All he ever does is read,
He's as useful as a dog lead.
He likes to vote,
And he reckons he can drive a boat.

Ryasat Khan (13)
Moseley School And Language College

RAW IS WAR

In every loud gunshot,
I distinguish people dying from a blood clot.
In every quiet, short night,
In every quiet, short night, I see a blinding light.

War is fighting with a stranger, it's not about leisure,
Which leads to graves and danger, not pleasure.
In every woman's cry, on a balcony,
I see a soldier sigh with thoughts of agony.

In every period of devastation,
There are kingdoms dying of starvation.
I observe a snake slide,
When soldiers are always denied.

War is always scandalous,
Victims are always ravenous.
War may lead to graves,
But soldiers so brave.

Zakar Hussain (15)
Moseley School And Language College

IS THE RAINFOREST PARADISE?

Far away there's a magical place,
Where animals are free,
And the trees are a rainbow of greens.
The stream is a glittering blue
And the plants are supreme.

Further in the rainforest,
The Amazon Indians are chopping trees
And their culture is ingenious.
The rainforest is a feast for the senses,
From the smallest monkey to the tallest emergent.

In the trees, birds cry out,
In the grass, jaguars pounce,
In the ground, snipers crouch,
In the canopy, flying squirrels swoop,
In the air butterflies flutter
And the rainforest is truly a paradise.

Lee Beasmore (13)
Moseley School And Language College

RAINFOREST

A tree here, a tree there,
Shades of green everywhere.
No blinking, no thinking,
You might miss something.
An iridescent macaw,
An irreplaceable millipede,
But please, just please,
Don't rip out those trees.
A plant may have a cure,
But if they go, I can't be sure.
If I look up and then look down,
I'm sure to be blasted with a sound.
There's mahogany, rosewood and greenheart,
These were here from the start.
They are beginning to fade out,
But what are we to do about
This?
We need the trees for paper, furniture
And the floorboards of the house.
But please, just please,
Don't rip down those precious trees.

Abida Butt (13)
Moseley School And Language College

The Asylum Cemetery

Ogling out of the window at the hilltop mausoleum,
It is an isolated, monotonous, sepulchre museum.
Graces buried in the vicinity of the haunted lair,
Soon, soon, soon you will be there.

Life is not mirth or the basis of dejection,
It is just a time of total passion.
Those who are orthodox, those who have that crypt,
They know one thing for sure; life is a diminutive script.

The conflicting bone and sinew in war
Assembles an appalling, bloody war.
The ambiance of combat, the hearts of carnage-phobia,
The flame of the phoenix, cannot be your death barrier.

Pandora's box, the curse of death,
When souls inhale a concluding breath,
Down in the necropolis, they immobilise and stare
At the spot where soon, soon, soon you will be there.

Akram Bahakinah (15)
Moseley School And Language College

My Poem

There's no one like my big, fat sister,
She acts just like a little creature.

She's got long, black hair
And she likes sleeping with a huge teddy bear.

She wears a massive round hat,
She is as tall as a cricket bat.

All she ever does is eat,
She's as useful as a loud drum beat.

She likes to record songs,
She reckons she's very strong.

Nasir Ali (13)
Moseley School And Language College

REMEDIAL NARCOTICS - DRUGS

I deserve best, I observe rest,
These victims are lacking platitude,
They are full of vindictive attitude.
This substance has the ability to intoxicate,
Like infectious bugs, not as fate.

People suffer from this thing,
It makes them delirious, uncanny and sing.
The zest and the rest,
Makes them tired, depressed, oppressed and distressed.

They must find this torment invigorating,
Their mind shouldn't be in this restraint,
These people agitate, complicate and don't hesitate,
They are delicate and are so gullible as bait.

Frequently these people cry,
Similarly, heavy rainfall would apply.
There is constant contradiction where their
Addiction will undoubtedly lead to valediction.
There should be a guide, a door, which leads to no more.

Faisal Farooqui (15)
Moseley School And Language College

WHAT IF . . .

Johnathan: What if . . .
I fell in the bathroom?

Stephanie: What if . . .
We go out to tea?

Darren: What if . . .
The teacher wasn't in?

Deepak: What if . . .
I lost my money?

Sukhbir: What if . . .
A bully came and punched me?

Shoib: What if . . .
Someone got me into trouble?

Lara: What if . . .
Somebody smashed my window at home?

Nick: What if . . .
The nurse wasn't in and there was an accident?

Nick: What if . . .
My dad was sick?

Sintero: What if . . .
I was good in the playground?

Janine: What if . . .
The food was cold?

Shoib: What if . . .
The builders never finish?

Stephanie: What if . . .
There is a fight at playtime?

Nick: What if . . .
What happened in America happens here?

What if . . ?

*Jonathan Pinfield, Stephanie Smith, Darren Evans, Deepak Kaura,
Sukhbir Singh, Shoib Khan, Lara Hall, Nicholas George,
Sintero Clarke, Janine James & Johnathan Keogh (14)
Selly Oak School*

SPIDERMAN

Spiderman, Spiderman, he is so great,
He is my mate.
Spiderman swings in the air and gets bad guys
And tries to get them in jail.
Spiderman gets villains too, like Mystereo,
Or Scorpion and Rhino, or Hydroman too.
Spiderman is the best,
Better than the rest,
He's the friendly neighbourhood Spiderman.

*Shane Ashman (11)
Selly Oak School*

HALF

There was a man who had half a car
And half a house, half of a chocolate bar
And half a back garden and half a book,
Half a dog and half a duck
And half a cat and half a hat.

*Paul Wright (11)
Selly Oak School*

JOURNEY THROUGH LIFE AS A FLOWER

Planted deep below, I was only a seed,
Would I be a flower or maybe a weed?
The rain fell down on uneven ground,
A few days later a bud was found.
Each day warmed by the great sun's shine,
My leaves unfold and my petals unwind.
Bright yellow in colour and smell of perfume,
As the bees pass by, they hum a sweet tune.
I hear footsteps coming closer, I am tugged from the ground,
I no longer hear nature all around.
In cold water upon my window sill,
My leaves are droopy, my petals are few,
Goodbye to you all, wish life was anew.

Charlotte Holden (13)
Shenley Court School

COMMUNITY IS MY MOM

She wears her hair up, all day long,
And never sings my favourite song.
She's loving and caring
And she's the one for sharing.
When it comes to love and community,
She's the one, you see.
I wish I could be as loving and caring as my mom.

I wish that one day, she will stop and see,
And then tell me all about community!
She's always there for me,
She always cares for me,
Oh I do love my mom, as you can see!

Rachel Williams (11)
Shenley Court School

THE JOURNEY

Journey with me now,
Hold my hand really tight
As we travel through these fields
This long and lonely night.

As we carry on moving,
We're never going to stop,
We'll travel all the way,
Until we reach the top.

And so we do continue
Down this long and winding lane,
For we have miles to travel, my friend,
Until we rest again.

So be a friend for me,
So alone I never travel
And as our journey's end is near,
I'm glad, my friend, that you were here.

Jason Vigers (13)
Shenley Court School

JAMAICA

I dream of going to Jamaica
To swim in the glistening sea,
To drink egg-nog and tall cocktails,
Under a coconut tree.

I dream of going to Jamaica,
I want to see a Rasta
Who lives in the middle of Jamaica.
That's my journey to Jamaica.

Richard Lynch (13)
Shenley Court School

WHAT IS COMMUNITY TO ME?

What is community to me?
Community to me is
A place that is safe,
No mugging, but hugging.
The community to me
Is a place for she and he,
Different races hang out
And play about.
Sanjay and Billy,
One Asian, one Caucasian,
Indians and Pakistanis
Get along with each other.
Jews and Palestinians
Make friends,
That is the community to me.

Billy Ashington (11)
Shenley Court School

THE JOURNEY OF A DROP OF RAIN

I'm starting my journey in the sea
With millions of droplets just like me.
The heat rises and I turn into water vapour,
As I get higher, I start to condense.
I get to my highest and then I am condensed.
In the air, I turn into a cloud, then the sky turns loud
From thunder and lightning in the shroud.
Then as rain I fall to the ground,
I swirl around and around.
I run into a stream and then into the sea,
With millions of droplets just like me.

Anthony Palmer (13)
Shenley Court School

MY JOURNEY POEM

Last week I went to Spain,
And I hoped it wouldn't rain.
The journey wasn't really long,
It was actually quite fun.
When I got there it was really hot,
So I had to buy a cool drink,
Then I went to my hotel, which was big,
And even had its own swimming pool.

The next day we went to the zoo,
'Cause my brother wanted to.
That day was really dull,
So the next day we did something fun.
At the end of the week we went home
To the coldness of sunny old England.

David Smith (13)
Shenley Court School

LOST AND FOUND

Come on home, come on home,
Where I can keep you nice and warm
With my love.

Now I have found you,
I will never let you go.
Come on home, come on home.

You can be safe and warm
And be with your family
Once again.

Sarah Ryan (12)
Shenley Court School

WHAT IS COMMUNITY TO ME?

Community to me is walking across the grove to call for my friends to go to school plus to hang or just to have fun.

Out of the bus window I can see people chatting to each other.

Children running to school and parents taking them to school.

People taking their dogs for a walk with smiles on their faces.

People sharing their feelings with family and friends.

An old lady giving children sweets, the children saying thank you, the lady said, 'Bless all of you children.'

A child fell over, he cut his leg and a kind
and caring man helped the boy up.

Community to me is people taking care of each other,
sharing, helping, being nice . . . that is community to me.

Gemma Tierney (11)
Shenley Court School

COMMUNITY POEM

The green grass and yellow flowers,
Because of our special powers.
The trees and bushes with the soft pace
As they see the smile on your face.

When someone sees your face,
They will enter you in any place.
When you act funny,
They think of you as sweet honey.

Sean Millard (11)
Shenley Court School

Journey Poem

It was my very first time on a plane,
I was scared, this was insane.
I could hear the propeller whizzing round,
I had never heard this kind of sound.
The plane was moving,
The trees passed by,
The plane took off,
It was very high.

We were now up in the air
And I stopped trembling in my chair.
I wasn't so scared anymore,
But it was beginning to be a bore.
Before I knew it, we hit the ground,
And the propeller stopped whizzing round.

Mark Jones (13)
Shenley Court School

Community

C ars are parked on the drives.
O ver miles of fields to play on, there's a park.
M e and my friend Matthew walk to school together.
M y best friend Sarah lives three doors away from me.
U p the road from me is a building called the I T
N ew people moved in yesterday
I n our road there's loads of children
T here are two fields by my house
Y esterday a car crashed on the big field.

Stacey Holland (11)
Shenley Court School

NOT WANTING TO UNDERSTAND!

I am always losing things,
Whether I'm far or near,
But have you ever lost someone,
Someone who called you dear?

It's hard when you lose someone,
'Cause you're suddenly full of fear,
As you watch all the adults sing
And fill themselves with beer.

Suddenly I feel a comforting hand,
And I turn round and see,
Someone also full of tears
Staring down at me.

They said to me you have to let go
And let what happened be,
They stared around the room,
Then walked towards my Auntie Dee.

There she lay, quiet and peaceful,
In an eternal, un-awakening sleep,
They're always saying, 'She's in a better place now,'
She'll go on without a peep.

I know right now I'm feeling sad,
But I know it will pass in time.
Every family has it too,
It's just standing in front of mine.

Natalie Farrell (13)
Shenley Court School

WHAT IS COMMUNITY?

What is community to me?
Seeing my friend down the street, he gave me a sweet.

What is community to me?
Seeing a cop who gave me a gun, then I shot someone,

What is community to me?
My friends cheering for me.

What is community to me?
I stroke my cat, it sees a rat and chases it down the street.

What is community to me?
Some clouds wondering past me.

What is community to me?
My friends are comforting me because I am sad as can be.

What is community to me?
Having a hamburger for tea.

What is community to me?
Going to the pictures to see Titan A E.

What is community to me?
A PlayStation is all I see, playing it on my TV.

What is community to me?
Going on English.co.uk, with adjectives and nouns are all cool.
That is community to me.

Richard Crow (11)
Shenley Court School

WHAT IS COMMUNITY TO ME?

What is community to me?
When I feel as cheerful as I can be!

What is community to me?
Playing, shouting, having fun with my friends.

What is community to me?
Just being around friends and family.

What is community to me?
Being at school, speaking with friends.

What is community to me?
Walking past the tall, green trees.

What is community to me?
Playing out, being sociable.

That's more than community to me!

Luke Noble (11)
Shenley Court School

COMMUNITY

C ars are zooming by
O ver the road are massive fields
M y house is across the road from Shenley Court
M y friends call for me in the morning
U p the road are some shops and a primary school
N ot many kids play outside in my area
I t has a massive conker tree over the road
T o get to school is not very far
Y oung people live in my area.

Nicola Kumas (12)
Shenley Court School

WHAT IS COMMUNITY TO ME?

Community to me
fills me with glee
because of all the people and friends,
when other people are happy
I'm happy
and all bad feelings mend.

Community to me
sometimes makes me feel lonely
when other people aren't around,
what makes me happy
is good friends and family
then I no longer feel down.

Rachel Hadley (12)
Shenley Court School

WHAT IS COMMUNITY TO ME?

What is community to me.
When you're feeling sad and lonely too,
All you really need is a friend to help you through.
A friend can help you through your toughest times,
Sometimes it can even make you rhyme.

Some people are good to me,
Some even help me pay a fee.
With community you can shed a tear
And sometimes you can share a beer.

That is what community means to me,
A nice box of chocolate
And a cup of tea.

Nicholas Graham (12)
Shenley Court School

MY JOURNEY

Long time ago
I had a journey,
A journey
That took me far and long,
So long, so long
Just to get me here.
I was so small when I began
As I moved my way around,
Round around around,
I began to get bigger and bigger.
Months later Mum and Dad
Found out what I was,
I was, I was a girl I say.
Today's the day, today's the day,
I was born, I was born,
I was born into this world.
My life began.
That's my journey, my journey,
My journey is now over.

Lisa Bick (13)
Shenley Court School

LIFE'S JOURNEY

My life is like a journey,
I travel further every day,
Sometimes I learn lots and lots
And sometimes go a little way.

I learn life's little secrets,
How to work and how to play,
How to be a good person,
In every single way.

On my way I meet people
And with them I am friends,
But for now I'll travel on my way
On my journey that never ends.

Judy Malin (13)
Shenley Court School

DEATH AND WAR

The rose petals drop to the floor
The sun slowly withers away
The darkness of death has come once again
War has come once again
All the tears and all the pain

Children cry
And women weep
For the loss of death has come today
All the silence stays in the world
All the soldiers stand so bold

The bombs are dropping
The guns are sounding
Discrimination and racism stays
The evils stands to glare
The scent of death is in the air

Wipe away the tears of the world
And do to people as you would
Like them to do to you.
Stop the killing and the threats
Say no to this hurt and pain
By violence what will the Earth gain.

Paul Dixie (14)
Shenley Court School

MY STORY

What is community to me?
Community is helping old ladies across the road
And giving money to a tramp.

What is community to me?
Community is buying old ladies their shopping
And doing the housework joyfully.

But when I am as happy as I can be
I feel like a bee buzzing merrily among the flowers
And nothing can get me out of this happy mood I'm in.

Anne-Marie Hockell (12)
Shenley Court School

COMMUNITY

I feel so sad without any friends
    What is community?
Who would be my friends?
    What is community?
I feel so sad without any friends to play with me.
    What is community?
Who would play with me?
    What is community?
I feel so happy that I've got friends to play with me
and to laugh and to tell jokes to each other.

Carlie France (11)
Shenley Court School

COMMUNITY (IN THE WORLD)

In the world there are lots of people,
Small, tall, white and coloured,
They are all part of a community.
You will never succeed by being nasty,
We are together and we should stick together.
What is community? It is people on Earth,
We have our own people in our life,
Some people get bullied and some people live in streets,
So community is the streets and the people.

Zara Ling (11)
Shenley Court School

THE BLACKBOARD

The blackboard sits on the wall
Dusty, old, dirty
Like an old shelf
Like an old pump bag on a peg
The blackboard sits alone
Unwanted, lonely, boring
Like an unwanted toy
Like a lonely person in a room
Like a boring day at home.
The blackboard sits behind the teacher's desk
Watched, unused, black.
Like a shop being watched
Like an unused carpet
Like a piece of black material
I feel as though I'm a bit like that.

Sarah Williams (12)
St Paul's School For Girls

SEASONS OF LOVE

    Seasons of love,
    Seasons of joy,
    Seasons of happiness
    And seasons of none.

Seasons changing from hot to cold
Water hot and water cold,
Drifting away into the sea,
Helpless as it survives the journey.
Going away and coming home,
Is it ever going to go for good.
The music of water going back and forth,
Where is it going,
When is it coming.
Oh where has it gone?
Has it disappeared into the air?
Is it coming back, I don't know.
If it would come back I would show it where to go.
Let's hope it comes back next year
And we can do it all over again.

Cecilia Smart (11)
St Paul's School For Girls

A POEM ABOUT AUTUMN

A year is divided into four seasons.
Autumn is one of them.
It makes me feel happy, it makes me feel awake.
It makes me feel lucky for I can see all the beautiful colours it has.

The reds, greens, oranges and brown,
From leaves which have fallen off a tree,
The wind's soft voice goes through my body
And makes my body tingle with freedom.

The sun is shining but not too bright
Between the band of blue and white skies.
As night falls the sun sets and its colours shine bright.

When morning comes I can hear the birds sing their joyful song.
I'm thankful for autumn because it makes me feel God's presence.

Tiisetso Mogase (13)
St Paul's School For Girls

MY GRANDAD WAS A LOLLIPOP MAN

He used to stand by the roadside each morning
and again at quarter to three
helping us to safely cross over when
when our parents couldn't see.

He'd give us a friendly smile or two
or used to say hello.
He'd walk over, warning cars to stop
so we would not be late.
We would all say thank you very much
and say we'd see you later, I hope.
When we came back out we'd all run down to see him.
He'd give me sweets if he had any to give.
He was the best lollipop man who was nice and kind,
I never felt lonely or sad,
I do miss him so 'cause he was the best grandad.

I wish he was still here now
I won't feel lonely or sad
but I think he's still here to keep me warm
every morning and night,
I think about him every night
'cause he was the best.

Stacey Winward (12)
St Paul's School For Girls

MY FRIENDS

My friends are always there for me,
Without them I don't know where I would be.

They make me laugh and make me giggle,
And even make my insides wriggle.

Sometimes I laugh when I'm not supposed to,
I laugh so much it hurts my nose.

When I fall out with my friends, we always get back together,
That's because I know we'll be friends forever.

I think my friends are really pretty,
Even when they're really witty.

I would never change my friends for the world,
Even the ones with curls.

We're mostly happy and hardly fight,
I think about it through the night.

Now you know about my friend,
And now you know it will never end.

Rachael Pallett (12)
St Paul's School For Girls

MOMS

Moms are great
Put food on your plate
Let you play with your mate
Make sure you have ate.

Moms are nice
Feed you with rice
Help you find a dice
Give you a drink of ice.

So treat your mom respectfully
Put food on her plate
Give her a drink with ice
Because she does it for you.

Moms should be proud
For what you have done
Moms be proud
Because we are proud of you.

Rachel Kane (11)
St Paul's School For Girls

MY BIG SISTER

My big sister has curly hair,
But she doesn't like any furry bear.
My big sister is very tall,
And her hobby is playing netball.
My big sister *really* talks,
But she doesn't like going for walks.
My big sister is very kind,
Even to me, she doesn't mind.
My big sister has lots of friends,
And they're always texting, send, send, send!
My big sister has a purple room,
And her music goes boom, boom, boom!
My big sister is very pretty,
And she loves playing with little Kitty.
My big sister loves watching TV,
But she keeps losing her front door key.
I love my sister and she loves me,
So we live very happily.

Maria Kenny (12)
St Paul's School For Girls

Autumn

Autumn is that time of year
when it shows that winter is nearly here.

Conkers fall off the trees to be gathered
by children searching on their knees.

Children run about
and scream and shout.

They love to play
all night and day.

Out come the gloves, hats and tights,
along with all the long, dark nights.

Winter is near
and Christmas is nearly here.

So now I am going to have fun
until I am done.

So bye-bye for now.

Catherine Harris (11)
St Paul's School For Girls

Seasons

Spring's out for quite a while,
Spring brings us a smile.
It makes us happy, it makes us stare
At the sunlight which is always there,
All we need now is a deckchair.

Summer's out and spring's gone,
The sun has stayed out still upon.
The bees are all here buzzing around,
Collecting the honey they have found.

Autumn has come, taking his crown,
Flashing leaves all around,
Throwing them on the ground.

Finally winter comes to take his place,
No sight of leaves are in trace.
Ice, frost and snow has come at a steady pace,
The snowmen are out with scarves and mittens,
Finally the snow has to go and spring comes again.
(Until next time).

Samantha Hawkins (11)
St Paul's School For Girls

MY CAT

My cat is fluffy and fat,
On his back I give a pat.
He has got his own bed,
Where he sleeps and where he's fed.
He follows me everywhere,
And anywhere I go,
But all the time I play with him and care,
And he has got lots of hair.
He is very special to me,
He plays with my teddy bee.
He goes out in the bushes
Even though he rushes.
He loves string,
He's always trying to catch birds' wings.
He always sleeps
And at night he creeps.

Laura O'Brien (11)
St Paul's School For Girls

POEM ABOUT AUTUMN

Leaves fall off trees,
All crispy and dry
Brown, yellow, orange, all different colours
As the leaves fall they crackle.

Autumn is a time for harvesting
Crops, food, wheat,
Trees blow side to side in the wind
Even bare trees blow in the wind.

People rushing through the leaves on the floor
All crackling
Even branches can fall off.

Leaves fall off trees,
All crispy and dry.
Brown, yellow, orange, all different colours
As the leaves fall they crackle.

Autumn is a colourful season.

Lauren Hall (12)
St Paul's School For Girls

TIGERS

Tigers are fierce,
Tigers are strong,
Tigers don't do anything wrong,
They lie there all day,
Waiting for their prey.

They are stripy as can be,
For all to see.
When they hunt their prey,
They sleep all day.

Tigers are my favourite animal,
Which all of you can see,
Tigers are the cutest things,
Just like you and me.

Tigers are the furriest things,
They like to hunt all day,
They also like to play.

Kelly Wyke (12)
St Paul's School For Girls

WINTER

Autumn has gone, winter is here,
The days are short, the nights are dark,
The snow starts to fall,
A thick, white blanket upon the floor.

It is coming up to Christmas now,
Hustle,
Bustle,
Round the shops,
Presents, sweets, sugar, spice
And all things nice.
Christmas is here
And the snow still falling.

Everyone's at Mass,
Everyone from class,
Including Mrs Tooked,
While at home the chicken was cooked.
At the end of Mass
Everyone rushed home for Christmas lunch
And washed it down with a glass of punch.
The snow's still falling and getting boring.

Victoria Barnett (11)
St Paul's School For Girls

MY FAMILY

There's Michaela, Katie, Mom, Dad and me
You're welcome to say we're a crazy family.
We all have our habits and I'm sure you do too,
Now sit back and listen, while I give you a quick view.

Mom's the cleaner and she's good at it too,
She feeds us and cleans us but there are arguments too.
She gets annoyed with Dad as he acts like a kid
By the way, he goes on about the cooking,
He couldn't cook for a pig.

Now there's Katie and Michaela, nine and four,
They're always arguing and bickering and wrestling on the floor.
Then when Michaela's crying she comes to me,
'Laura, Laura, Katie just hit me!'

Now as for me and Katie you don't wanna know,
Running around the house, *ready steady go!*
Swinging down stair banisters,
Watch out below!

Now that's my crazy family!

Laura Kielty (11)
St Paul's School For Girls

SEASONS

Spring has gone, summer is here,
It's the season which is the best,
It's the season with the longest day;
The 21st June.
Lovely green grass starts to appear,
From winter which has lots of snow
Falling from the sky,
To spring which has the newborn and
Now we are here in the summer once more.

It's summer, the best 'cause you can go
To the beach, the shops, the sea,
The beautiful sunset, how can you resist,
The lovely gum and the sweets.
That's all I've got to say about the wonderful summer.

Ruth Guy (11)
St Paul's School For Girls

MY LOVE

The way she walks and swings her hair
The way she looks she tries to care
I know that I will never see
A gracious jumper such as she
She could jump higher than you and me

Then one day we were out in the woods
She fell over some horrible goods
So from that day her walk was gone,
Her jump was lost, that special one.

She was my love until that day,
She would not jump or run or play
My heart it felt like it was lost
I did not care about the cost.

She soon grew old and I knew she was ill
I knew she was dying with all my will,
So my greatest friend was gone in a flash
My soul burnt into ash.

I miss her when I think back
Love for her I do not lack
And here I am remembering the source
Of my beautiful imaginary horse!

Hayley Williams (12)
St Paul's School For Girls

MY BEST FRIEND

My best friend is called Leah
She is sitting right here.
She has good looks,
And loves Harry Potter books.

She has a cat,
That eats a lot of rats.
She has a guinea pig,
That looks as if it wears a wig.

Her sister is called Jessie,
She is awful messy.
Leah's really clever,
And is as light as a feather.

She is a great best friend,
I hope our friendship never ends.
She is really caring,
But is never swearing,
That's my best friend, Leah.

Kayleigh Sheridan (12)
St Paul's School For Girls

SUMMERTIME

Summer is here at last,
The smell of freshly cut grass,
Oh look! The ice cream van is here,
Summer is the best time of year.
The heat of the blazing sun,
Brings the smile to the face of everyone,
The yellow golden sand
Runs smoothly out of my hand.
T-shirts, vests and shorts,
Oh how I longed for those long summer nights,
Where you can stop out late and have water fights.

The newly fresh green leaves,
Summer is about to drift away,
Oh how I wish it really would stay,
Time to wrap up warm now winter is near,
Summer is definitely the best time of the year!

Roxanne Boothe (11)
St Paul's School For Girls

MARMALADE

He's buried in the bushes
with dock leaves round his grave.
A crime cat desperado
and his name was Marmalade.
He's the cat that caught the pigeon
that stole the neighbour's meat . . .
and tore the velvet curtain
and stained the satin seat.
He's the cat that spoilt the stew
and chased the lady's poodle
and scratched her daughter too . . .

But . . .

No more will you hear his cat flap
or scratches at the door
or see him at the window
or hear his catnap snore

So . . .

Ring his grave with pebbles
erect a noble sign
for here lies Marmalade
and Marmalade was mine!

Siobhan Hussain (12)
St Paul's School For Girls

WINNIE THE POOH

I love Winnie The Pooh,
Books, pictures, videos too,
Bedspreads, toys to mention a few.

Winnie The Pooh,
Full of life,
So soft and cuddly,
He's so round and so bubbly.

His friends are many,
Christopher Robin,
Piglet, Eeyore, Tigger too,
Rabbit, Gopher, Kanga and Roo.

He's got a big tummy
Because he loves his honey,
He eats so much it makes him funny.

Laura Taylor (11)
St Paul's School For Girls

SUPER DOG

Superman's dog, he's the best
Better than all the rest
Helping pets in distress
SD on his chest.

With super sight
He'll take you for a flight.
He's very strong
And never wrong.

Do not worry
He's always about
When you're in trouble give him a shout
He'll help you no doubt.

Superman's dog - bionic sent
Crime prevention - his intent
Woof and tough - cement he'll dent,
What's his name . . . Bark Kent!

Clare Stajka (11)
St Paul's School For Girls

THE SEASONS

I like spring when new life starts to grow.
To see bulbs shooting through the ground.
Daffodils standing tall and proud.
The pink of the blossom and the fresh smell of newly-cut grass.

I like autumn when the animals hibernate for winter.
Squirrels scurrying for nuts and food.
Golden yellows, reds and browns.

I like winter when the nights are dark and the days are cold and crisp.
I love to see snowdrops glistening in the sky like sparkles of glitter.

I like summer best of all, when the days are longer.
The golden sands of beaches.
The sun glistening on the cool, blue sea.
The smell of summer flowers in a rainbow of beautiful colours.
The warmth of the sun smiling down on the world.

Hayley Hulme (12)
St Paul's School For Girls

THE MIDSUMMER BALL

It was midsummer,
There was a ball,
I was promised to be taken by Paul,
Paul was tall,
He sat me on a stall,
And told me,
Look here, you see,
I was once
A buzzing bee,
I went to tea,
By the sea,
Where Madam Lee,
Changed me into a he.
Here I am next to you,
Do you still love me,
Because I love you too.

Michelle Cave (12)
St Paul's School For Girls

SEASONS

Spring is new life, baby animals are born,
Spring is fresh, crisp and dry,
Spring is the start of something new,
Spring is new leaves on very tall trees.

Summer is the sun, way up in the sky,
Summer is lazy, sunbathing all day,
Summer is warm so keep yourself cool,
Summer is time to go to the beach and play in the sea.

Autumn is leaves falling from trees,
Autumn is golden and brown,
Autumn is rakes picking up leaves.
Autumn is bonfires and Hallowe'en too.

Winter is cold,
Winter is hats, scarves and gloves.
Winter is snow falling from the sky,
Winter is Christmas, so ho, ho, ho!

Sally Wagstaff (11)
St Paul's School For Girls

UNDER THE FLOORBOARDS

Under the floorboards
a creature lives
it oozes full of slime
it loves to watch Prime Time.
Its belly rumbles
and it mumbles
'I need to have my tea.'
It creeps through the cracks
and finds its snacks
a guitar for starters
and then a rotten chocolate bar.
It oozes out the front door
and at midnight it is back
with oil on its back
and an old dirty rag
and a teddy in its hand.

Hannah Smith (13)
St Paul's School For Girls

SEASONS OF THE YEAR

Grey and black
Transforms the sky
As if the world
Is about to die

But then a bud pops out of the ground
As if it was lost but then was found
April showers soon fly by
It's the end of winter, goodbye, goodbye.

The sun comes out
It will stay, I dare not doubt
Laughter and screams
And time for ice creams.

Red and yellow and orange and brown
All the leaves fall down to the ground
Now it's time to go back to school
It's a long time now 'til April's fool.

This time is full of fun and joys
'Specially when it comes to toys
But let's not forget it's true celebration
Say a prayer for peace all over the nation

It's now back to grey and black
And freezing Ice Jack will soon be back
But the new year will soon fly by
We will have fun again, my oh my.

Aimee Kelly (11)
St Paul's School For Girls

WORDS

Words can be hurtful
Words can be mean
They can make you sad and feel bad
Others can be kind, gentle and sweet
They can make you feel loved
Which everyone needs.
Words are feelings which everyone has
Some are good and some are bad
They twirl around in your head
Then come together to be said
Every day words come out of your mouth
Big ones, small ones, some hard to pronounce
We don't take much notice of the words we say
Which is why people get hurt more and more each day.

Lisa McCarthy (13)
Stockland Green School

THE WIND

On a cold winter's day
The wind seems to say
People think I'm no fun
You can only have that in the summer's sun
But come over here and see
Just how much fun I can be
You can spend all day in a puddle
Or keep warm with a cuddle
But the best fun of all
Is when the snow of winter starts to fall.

Nicola Groom (13)
Stockland Green School

WINNING DOESN'T MATTER

I'll win
What I've wanted to win.
Today is the big race.
I will run with all my might.
I will put up a good fight.
Hopefully I'll be in first place.

I'm losing, I won't quit
Because quitters are losers.
Competing should be the best prize of all
No matter what your size.
You could be taller, smaller, thinner or fatter
Winning shouldn't matter.
If people are calling you a loser
Just laugh in their face
Because at the end of the day you were
                              in the race.

John Leachman (13)
Stockland Green School

MEMORIES

Some memories are good, some are bad,
Some make you happy, some make you sad.
Some grow better given time,
Some disappear one at a time.

Good memories you can never forget,
The bad ones are the ones you regret,
Memories stay with you,
In everything you do.

No one can be lonely,
When they've got their memories.
Memories are something you hold in your heart.
Memories and you will never part.

Gemma Stratford (13)
Stockland Green School

THE FEELINGS INSIDE

As I look outside I see,
People without a care,
Some clever,
Some who love a dare
And some happy.

All these feelings and emotions,
I feel inside are empty,
If you look inside you can see confusion,
Different things,
Different illusions,
But all I ask is for love and attention,
With happiness
And a lot of affection.

I look outside one more time,
To see nothing but trees.
Some yellow,
Some green
And some even red.

Then I think to myself how would
My feelings look inside?

Danielle Radway (13)
Stockland Green School

SEPARATIONS

In our world,
There are many things that separate us
                         from each other.
But do these differences really matter,
And should we take any notice of them?

Many people differ in religion,
But does it really matter if you're Christian,
                         Muslim or Catholic?
Many arguments have been caused over religion,
But if you listen closely, God is calling for peace.

Many people differ in race,
But does it matter if you're Asian, African
                         or English?
But these differences can cause a lot of racism,
Yet we could all be related in some way.

Does it really matter if you're fat or skinny,
If you're tall or short,
Or if you're pretty or ugly?
Isn't it what's on the inside that counts?

Does it really matter if you're cool or not,
If you're confident or shy,
Or if you're fashionable enough . .?
I don't think it does!

Should we judge,
And label each other due to appearance?
Should there be status in our society,
Or should we all be known as important as the other?

Do you think we should let these differences separate us?
I don't think we should.
I think we should all be know as human beings,
And *unite* in the world together!

Kimberley Bradley (13)
Stockland Green School

SPLIT PERSONA

I've got a split persona
I act differently in front of others,
Make myself look better
Lie if necessary
I do it to look good.

I've got a split persona
I behave differently in front of others
I act mouthy, upfront, sometimes I act
Really mean, I don't mean to
I do it to look good.

I've got a split persona
I dress differently in front of others
I get the most fashionable before the most practical
I get the most expensive rather than the cheapest
I do it to look good.

I've got a split persona
But you know what, I don't want one
I just want to be me, Morgan Webley
Nothing more, nothing less, just me.

Morgan Webley (13)
Stockland Green School

I CAN'T WRITE POEMS

I can't write poems to save my life.

C an't write poems I'm such a dud
A ny poems are impossible to write
N o chance in hell
T o write a poem that will be good.

W rite poems, wrong poems, good poems,
                bad poems I cannot tell
R eading or writing it's all too hard
I write poems they sound like a blur
T o even think of poems makes me sick
E ven at school when I write poems I pray
                for the bell.

P oems, who needs them anyway?
O nly a bunch of words that rhyme
E veryone's good at writing poems
M e, well I'm no good at writing anything
S o that's my attempt at writing a poem.

Liam McGuinness (13)
Stockland Green School

DAVE AND SCHOOL

There was a young man called Dave,
Who didn't know how to behave,
He was bad at French and drama,
And brought in his pet iguana.

Yellow slips, red slips and detentions
And other matters that I cannot mention.
Dinner time is alright,
Football, tennis, foods and fights.

Sitting waiting for the bell to ring,
Watching the drama students dance and sing.
So this is the end of Dave and school,
For one thing school's not cool.

Sean Allen (13)
Stockland Green School

THE PLANE CRASH
(Dedicated to the victims of the plane crash in America)

Imagine sitting on a plane knowing you're going to die,
Trying to find a phone so you can say your last goodbyes.
Phoning the people you love so much,
Knowing you will never again feel their touch.
Holding on to memories so dear,
Wishing your loved ones were near.
You start to cry as you hear their voice,
Knowing you have no choice.
You're going to die.

As the plane reaches the building you don't know what to do,
Filled with emotion you wish your loved ones were here too.
Wishing you could give your family one last kiss,
Hoping that the plane will miss.
As the plane hits the building you know you have no choice,
Your face winces as you hear a screaming voice.
You wish you could see your family once more
Before the building hits the floor.
You know you have no choice,
You're going to die.

Laura Higgins (13)
Stockland Green School

LIFE

Life!
Is it just a four letter word
Or can it mean what you want it to mean?
Is it anything or anyone like you and me?
Is it the colours of the rainbow
Or the birds in the trees?
My definition of life is,
People,
Running, playing,
Joining together as one.
Life!
What comes to mind when you say this word?
Could it be the air we breathe?
Is it the past, present or future?

Marteen Savory (14)
Stockland Green School

LOVE

What is love?
What can it be?
It so amazes me.
Is it good?
Is it bad?
I don't know, I'll wait and see.

Am I too young to understand?
Is love all that grand?
Will it be what I want it to be?
One day I'll be able to see.

I want to know what it feels like,
I want to know what it is like,
I want to know what it can be like,
To be loved.

Katie Fowler (13)
Stockland Green School

CAR CRASH

I was driving in my car one day
I drove really far away.
I said, 'Hey, something's strange, strange.
Hmmm that tastes really fizzy
Ouch I feel really dizzy.
Ahhh I've crashed
And everything's smashed
And I am crouched like a duck
Which means I am stuck.
Can someone help me?
I am all alone
With no phone
With no one to contact
Who would come immediately
To see if I am alive
And to save me
From the nasty crash?

Anton L Williams (12)
Stockland Green School

COLOURS

A band of bright marigold,
A warm glow of ivory,
A jazzy rain of scarlet,
All kinds of colours.
A jeer of shimmering gold,
A jamboree of jade and violet,
A lacklustre of blacks and greys,
All kinds of colours.
A disco of dancing blues
Acquainted by a blushing magenta
And last but not least a triumphant
Cast of orange to brighten up a day.

Karine Stevenson (14)
Stockland Green School

RAINDROPS, RAINDROPS

Splash they go on the floor, *splish, splash, splish.*
Splash they're falling from the sky,
Big ones, small ones they're every single where,
Wetting people's rooftops, wetting people's cars.
If you hear the sound *splish, splosh* run inside your house.
Drip, drip, drip, drop the sun begins to appear
Raindrops, raindrops have gone away,
Maybe they'll come back another day
When it's not so cold and the sun begins to warm us up.

Shyro Lall (12)
Stockland Green School

A Football's Life

I don't like being a football
we play on muddy grounds.
I want to be a volleyball
and bounce on the soft sand.

I am black and blue with bruises too
and I'm always on the ground.
I get kicked up the wall
just because I'm a football.

I don't want to be a football
or a rugby ball too.
Those sports are too rough for me
I prefer to be a pot of glue.

The football match is coming
and my shape is flat.
I don't want to be a football,
I want to be a cat.

So as I'm here on the football pitch
I've got a few words to say.
I'm glad to be a football
on this rainy day.

James Maiden (12)
Stockland Green School